D1483192

PUT THAT IN WRITING

□ *PUT* □
THAT IN
WRITING

||||||||||||||||||||||||||||||||||||||||||||||||||||||||||||||||

■ by Jonathan Price ■

||||||||||||||||||||||||||||||||||||||||||||||||||||||||||||||||

VIKING

VIKING

Viking Penguin Inc., 40 West 23rd Street,
New York, NY 10010, U.S.A.
Penguin Books Ltd, Harmondsworth,
Middlesex, England
Penguin Books Australia Ltd, Ringwood
Victoria, Australia
Penguin Books Canada Limited, 2801 John Street
Markham, Ontario, Canada L3R 1B4
Penguin Books (N.Z.) Ltd, 182–190 Wairau Road,
Auckland 10, New Zealand

First published in 1984 by Viking Penguin Inc.
Published simultaneously in Canada

LIBRARY OF CONGRESS CATALOGING IN PUBLICATION DATA
Price, Jonathan, 1941–
    Put that in writing
    1. Commercial correspondence.   2. Business report
writing.   3. Memorandums.   I. Title.
HF5721.P74   1984   808'.066651   83-40256
ISBN 0-670-79149-0

Printed in the United States of America by
R. R. Donnelley & Sons Company, Harrisonburg, Virginia
Set in Bodoni Book

□ *CONTENTS* □

□ *Introduction* □

||||||||||||||||||||||||||||||||||||||||||||||||||||||||||||||||||||||||||||||||||||||

I n business, we write to get something accomplished, to persuade people to:

- give us their votes, their approval, their support;
- okay our plans—and budgets;
- send money for our group, product, or company;
- ask us in for job interviews;
- carry out our orders—in the right way, at the right time.

And when nothing much happens, we suspect that fuzzy writing may have blurred our point, made us look dumb, gotten us ignored. We see money, promotions, and fame go to the people who write well—in part, because their writing gets more done.

But most of us were trained in school to write badly—to use big words, to hide our point (or lack of point), to fill up pages even when we've run out of things to say, to make simple matters sound complex. That is what most of us got A's for.

Unfortunately, in business that kind of writing just causes confusion. Some people read it, and throw it in the wastebasket. Others glance at it, and say they'll get to it next week. A few read it and misunderstand it, or misinterpret it to their own advantage. You send it out, and nothing comes back. That's the sign of schoolbook writing: no results.

The style that gets the most work done is plain. We recognize it when we see it. The writer gets to the point—fast. We hear a real human being talking to us. We don't have to translate a lot of jargon to get at the meaning. The message is short but clear.

You'll find a plain style pays off for your company and for you. Your readers will be able to:

- spot a problem, without having to figure it out themselves;
- know who did what, without struggling with gobbledygook;
- understand what you recommend immediately—no need for extra questions or more reports;
- act on time, rather than having to go back for further study;
- appreciate your making their job easier;
- recognize you as forthright and decisive—a good candidate for promotion.

It's not easy to learn to write in this way, particularly if you've been badly taught. You might have to spend a year strengthening your style. The process resembles getting your body in shape: you have to keep at it, but after a while, you feel better. As you write, you no longer feel angry, frustrated, confused, guilty, and anxious. You just say what you mean.

The first part of this book will help you develop a plain style—writing that means business. So if you're ready for a complete retooling, start at the beginning, and browse on through. The rest of the book will help you with particular writing tasks such as letters, reports, and memos. So if you have an immediate project, skip to the appropriate chapter for specific tips. I've designed these chapters to get you going fast, with practical ideas you can act on—not just think about.

I'm a professional writer, but I've worked as an employee and consultant in large corporations for six of the last dozen years. I've been a consultant, trainer, technical writer, and supervisor, responsible for budgets from $100,000 to $1,000,000. In the process, I've taught about a thousand people how to write reports, seven hundred to prepare résumés, a few hundred technical writers to create computer manuals, and dozens of top executives to write memos that produce action. This book is a summary of the ideas I used to help these people improve their writing.

Throughout the years, one idea kept emerging as the most important: to write better you must develop your taste for truth. You have to pay more attention to what you really think, feel, see, and want.

You'll need the courage to discard various false fronts you acquired in school and on the job. When you say what you really mean and report what you've actually done, you'll find you write faster because you're not flim-flamming, fancy-talking, or fogging. In short, to clear up your prose, avoid lying.

It sounds simple, but it takes years to learn: say what you really think. You'll get more done.

▪ A Plain Style ▪

□ *START NOW* □

||||||||||||||||||||||||||||||||||||||||||||||||||||||||||||||||||||||||||||

Start writing by thinking, not wrestling with words. That way you can put off writing for a while. And when you begin your first sentence, you'll have a lot more to say.

If you worry about the way you never quite get around to writing until it's almost too late, you should ask yourself why everything else gets done first. Most people who postpone writing do so out of fear, anger, or sheer damn laziness. You

4

may be afraid of being turned down, rebuffed, rejected. Angry at having to do the report; angry at the boss; angry at the people you're addressing. Frightened of taking a stand. Depressed at the idea of thinking the subject through, and coming to a conclusion. Convinced you'll never be a good enough writer. Exhausted by all that anticipated work.

Most people put off writing. If you put it off too long, the writing suffers, because when you rush at the last moment, you write too much, and you only find out what you think on the last page. But then it's too late to go back and help the reader by putting the point at the beginning. You lose any chance to edit, to clarify, to cut out embarrassing excesses. The earlier you start, the better. But don't start any business writing with your first sentence.

First, set up a schedule. Figure out when your work is due, and then decide to finish it a week or so earlier. Having an advance deadline means you have some leeway, toward the end. And it's always at the end of a project that you run into delays, extra charts to draw, new sections to add. Also, when you're running late, machines know it, and break down. When you have a few days to get a report typed, copied, and distributed, downtime doesn't mean disaster.

Also, set a time when you're going to stop doing research, and start writing—otherwise you may con yourself into thinking you're working on the report when you're actually just browsing around for stray facts.

Estimate the hours this task will take. One way to gauge this is to figure about how many pages the final product will be, and then multiply that by two, three, or four hours. Most people underestimate by half the time it takes to write a report. That's because they don't count preliminary research, typing, copying, revising, editing. Here are rough guidelines:

- For a complicated project that must win approval from several people before "going public," you may need four hours for each final page.

- For a simple report on a subject you know well, you'll need about two hours a page.
- For an important memo, allow *at least* an hour. (Most people imagine they write memos in five minutes.)

Then block out that time on your calendar. This signals your unconscious mind that you really intend to do the project—and it will help you later when you need to fend off other demands on your time. Most people imagine that writing is like talking on the phone; you just do it. But writing is work, and it deserves the same respect you give meetings and interviews—a place on your schedule.

Next, try writing down what your main point will be, in a sentence, not just a subject. It's easy to say that you will write "something about earnings," but harder to say "I will show that earnings have fallen due to labor costs and financing charges." You need a point, not just a topic; and sentences convey complete ideas, where phrases merely hint at them. Here are some test-runs for a main point:

- We need to put our sales demos on videodisks because they let you go right to the part you want.
- We should put the demos on videodisks because they are TV, but TV that can be controlled by the sales-people, so customers only see the part that applies.
- We should put our sales demos on videodisks.

You may not find the perfect expression of your main idea. That's okay. At this stage, what you need is a general idea. It shows your unconscious mind what you're aiming at. Now that you've set a date when you're going to start writing, your unconscious will go off and meditate on that idea.

This works even when you have only five minutes to spare. Instead of scribbling, then, take some deep breaths, calm your tense muscles, relax. Then envision the completed work. Imagine what it will look like, how much it will weigh, what its title will be. Imagine handing it to your readers. Imagine their congratulations, and signatures on checks. Tell your mind calmly, "This is what I'm after." Then forget it for a few minutes. Clean your desk. Sharpen pencils. Read some good prose.

That is starting without actually starting. Instead of getting lost in a maze of words, you're using your dreaming mind to flesh out an idea, organize sections, refine your argument— before you write.

□ *FIGURE OUT WHOM YOU'RE TALKING TO* □

W ho's talking to whom? Many business letters end up trampled underfoot because the writers didn't know or care about the people they were talking to. Common sins include: treating old hands as beginners, or overwhelming beginners with advanced material; forgetting to tell readers what they need to know, or filling them in—at length—on what they already know; and assuming that every reader has a burning desire to read on.

No co-workers *have* to read what you write, even if it's related to their jobs. They'll pretend they read it; they'll tell you they have; but their actions may show they have no idea what you wrote. If that's happened to you, consider whether you were addressing them directly.

Sometimes you have several audiences. If possible, write to each separately: prepare one report for experts, another for new employees. If that's not possible, then at least put a note up front telling each group what to read and what to skip.

No matter which audience you're addressing, you'll need to

understand them. Really think about them. If you already know them, go beyond the demands of business. What are these people really like? The clearer the picture you form of your audience, the more you'll be able to interest them in what you have to say.

Here are some questions to ponder:

- How old are they?
- How rich?
- How experienced in this job?
- What occupations have they had in the past?
- What are they afraid of?
- What angers them most?
- What are they proud of?
- What do they want at home and on the job?
- How will your ideas help them?
- What suspicions might they have about your ideas?
- Have they got some good reasons not to want to hear what you say?
- How much do they know about this subject?
- How much do they *want* to know—if anything?
- Why will they read this?

As you think about the readers, you may find you feel more emotions than you expected. That's natural. You may notice traces of contempt. (Why do they need another report; can't they see?) Or boredom. (Why do I have to do another report?) Or fear. (I hope they don't catch on.) Or rage. (These bastards better approve this budget or I'm going over to the competition.) Don't try to repress those feelings. Repressing them now just means they'll pop up later in your tone. People will read what you've written, and feel vaguely uncomfortable. They may not be able to pinpoint why they get mad reading your report, but the hostility hidden there will come across.

Write down what you think about the readers. Then save that paper in a file where no one else will ever see it, or toss it away. You'll be amazed how easy it will be to write to them afterward. Your feelings may still emerge as you write, but you'll have more control over them. You may even feel a little sympathy for the readers.

As you begin outlining your report, anticipate your readers' reactions. Try to imagine them asking: but what good is it? What's it to me? But can you prove that? So what do you want me to do about it?

In this way, you'll be able to answer objections before they grow into wholesale rejection. Your writing will seem like part of a conversation, not a lecture.

Some people, when writing, like to dictate as if the readers were about to receive the tape, not a transcript. Pace the floor and point, if that helps. Talk to pictures of your audience. Anything that helps you imagine you're talking to someone helps your writing. But don't leave it to your secretary to make sentences out of gasped phrases. That's unfair and a bit risky—it leaves your meaning up for grabs. Furthermore, that habit can lead you into double-tone—directing some thoughts to your secretary, others to the recipient. Result: an air of indecision or duplicity.

Clear writing is not just talk put into ink. It has fewer false starts (they've been edited out), less meandering around the point, tighter structure. It has no sound, no body, no social ambiance; with writing, you have to do it all with words. But if you have a realistic picture of your audience, your writing can echo some of the friendliness and effectiveness of ordinary conversation.

□ *MAKE SMART NOTES* □

When you dig into your material, you're clearing the ground for your writing. You'll save time—on memos, letters, even reports—if you know the general shape of your argument in advance.

Start by sketching out your foundations in a very rough outline. Ask yourself these questions:

- What's your main idea? Say it in one sentence, beginning "I think . . ."
- What subjects will you have to mention?
- What are the major sections? Possible minor ones?

- Roughly, what comes first, second, third in importance?

Then figure what kind of supporting evidence you need, such as quotes, dates, prices, statistics, specifications, ideas. By making up this outline you get a feel for the kind of information you want to turn up in your research. Maybe you have it all in your files, maybe not. But right now you want a list of everything you need in order to construct your report.

Most people waste time taking notes on side issues, interesting detours into irrelevant material. They browse through files that relate only to the most minor points, neglecting to find evidence for their main thesis. Some people get too detailed, others remain too general in their comments. Then when they come to write, they discover that their notes don't apply.

Note-taking is active thinking. By keeping your mind on what you want to prove, you can take notes that will help you in the writing. You can avoid a lot of unnecessary research by asking this question of every new book, interview, or study: how does this help me say what I want to say?

Put each quote you need on a separate sheet of paper, or, better yet, an index card. Label it with the topic this note refers to. And add your comments, so that later you won't have to think them all out a second time. When you actually get down to writing, you'll find some of your topics meld or split in two; that's when the cards make it convenient to rearrange your evidence without scissors and paste.

Don't be bashful, either. Ask librarians to help; they love to, and almost no one asks them. Call experts. Talk to everyone who's involved, no matter what their position.

When you interview someone, start off with a list of questions designed to raise every major topic you're going to be writing about. Then let the discussion wander. In general, try to find out what they think before you let them know where you stand—otherwise, they may tailor their remarks to suit your purposes, and you may miss out on some valuable new ideas.

If you have time, consider questionnaires. Take the time to frame your questions in a neutral way—avoid giving away your position. The effort of devising the questions will help you articulate your ideas, too. When creating a questionnaire, keep it short—one or two pages. Leave plenty of room for answers. Write a cover letter, or paragraph, explaining why you want the information, what you will do with it, and how their responses will be kept confidential. And test the questions out on half a dozen people before sending them out—you'll find that what seemed perfectly clear to you can get interpreted three or four different ways.

Whatever you do, take a lot of notes. You'll discard two-thirds of them when you write, but you will be able to choose the most poignant quotation, the most dramatic statistics, the irrefutable fact. Without a lot of notes, you have to settle for whatever you've stumbled on, and usually that's not very impressive.

Now you have to take notes on your notes. As you review this mass of material, keep revising your original rough outline. You'll see that some points are now much less important than you thought, while others that you didn't even think of originally turn out to be crucial. Take some time to reconsider your main point, too. Does it still seem true? How could you modify it, so it's more acceptable, more comprehensive, more precise? Can you make it shorter, without changing the essence of what you want to say?

As you approach the end of your research—the day you've decided to stop studying and start writing—make time to sit and shuffle your cards. Sort out your notes by topic, and see which topics end up with no cards. Which stacks tower above the others? Perhaps those can be divided up into smaller topics.

You can now begin to see the scale of your report: which parts will be large, which small, how long the whole may be.

You may also get a glimpse of a structure that will connect these topics, an overall organization, in which one topic logically comes before another, and one idea clearly outweighs another, and all lead to your carefully prepared conclusion.

Yes, all this takes time. But it makes the actual writing go faster. You'll have thought through the material from so many different angles that you know just how to present it. You'll have encountered most of the objections to your position, and learned how to disarm them. You'll have refined your main point so well that you don't have to change it as you go. You'll avoid a lot of painful revisions.

The better the notes, the easier the writing.

☐ *REORGANIZE AROUND YOUR MAIN IDEA* ☐

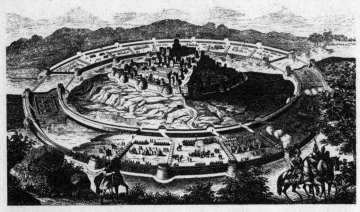

Your main point acts as a citadel you defend, a central image around which you build the rest of your report, an intelligence behind it all—the meaning.

Almost every business communication should have a point to make. Even when people tell you to "just write up the facts," they want you to digest the data, and take a stand. What does it all mean?

Unfortunately, most reports come out disorganized. They begin with apologies, acknowledgments, background, and other forms of hemming and hawing. They finally touch on the main point at about page five. Then they skitter away from it so quickly that the readers rarely realize that's the message. Some reports look as if the author had no opinion at all. Most leave the reader wondering what to do next.

So before you write the report, ask yourself:

    1. What is the main idea I want my reader to agree to?

2. What do I want the reader to do after finishing this?
   (Imagine an action, not a mood.)

Keep testing your main point to see if it's really what you want to say. Put it in this form: "I think this: . . . ," and then add a complete sentence, with an active verb, not some form of *to be*. Like this:

I think this: We should tear down Building 14.
I think this: You should approve the Smithson contract this week.
I think this: Our European competitors are beating the hell out of us in Germany.

Not like this:

This report deals with the facilities issue.
Cost savings are always very important.
I've just gotten back from my trip to Japan.

All your other ideas should be marshalled to support this main point—or dropped. Group your notes under the ideas that will back up your idea, then put those groups in some order. Here are some familiar ways to put your writing in some sort of order:

- Largest, medium, smallest
- Most impressive, least
- Most effective, least
- Most urgent, least
- General, particular, general
- Cause, effect
- Appeal to self-interest, demonstration of benefits, clincher

Since everyone recognizes these organizing principles, you make your report easier to digest when you choose one of them.

Within each group of notes, adopt *some* organizing principle. And within each topic, do the same. Make sure you feel comfortable with your overall organization before you start writing. You'll save yourself hours of cutting and pasting.

Yes, you should have an introduction and a conclusion. But these should emphasize your main point, and they should hint at the way you've organized the report as a whole. A conclusion does not have to sum up *everything* that went before— just your ideas, and a clear statement of what you want the reader to do about them.

Don't overorganize, however. If you have more than three major sections (not including introduction and conclusion), you're risking confusion. If you have more than three layers of heading, you're getting finicky.

As you begin each paragraph, ask yourself how this material will build your case. If the connection seems thin, maybe you should skip the subject.

A strong organization shows an aggressive mind at work. So bully those facts into line, make them work together to show off your central thesis—and defend it.

☐ *GET TO THE POINT—FAST* ☐

A n idea has an edge to it. Sharpen that edge and strike with it.

Like a knife blade, an intellectual point has two main parts. At first glance, a stranger may just see the flash of the subject. That's the steel. Close up, though, he can feel the particular angle you take. That's the cutting edge.

Don't waste time with some long, slow buildup. Yes, it shows you've done your homework, and you're a razzle-dazzle twirler of words. But where's the point? Leave suspense for the movies.

Skip the history lessons, too. Who cares about every letter that preceded this one? If that kind of endless background is important (which I doubt), bury it in the body of your report or in an appendix.

Too many people blunt their message for goody two-shoes reasons. For instance, some people learned in school that they shouldn't claim anything until after they've proved it. So they make the hapless reader wait until they've gotten all their evidence together—somewhere past page 51. Writers who feel guilty about what they are reporting figure that they can wear out the reader, or hide the bad news under fifteen pages of preparatory matter. Other writers feel so humble about their opinions that they bury the idea under bushels of printout. That way, if you insist on knowing what they think, you're forced to read every page, and wonder all the way.

Think what happens to the readers, then. Some doze off. Others drift away from the writer's obscure point, and imagine another. A few get mad. Several waste an hour sweating out the meaning, then wonder why the writer made it so hard to find.

So put your message in your title, if possible. Even after a "Dear Sir," you can toss in your main idea—not just your subject—like this:

Dear Sir:

We've found your lost check #132.

Yes, put it in your first sentence. Devote your first paragraph to it. In the first page take time to sketch out its magnitude, its value, and its possible consequences. But start with the point.

DON'T START WITH THE SLOW CURVE

Since the invention of movable type, there have been collectors of books. Here at the Company Library, we have been privileged to inherit the collections of many rare spirits. Our technology trove is world renowned. We take great pride in our periodical file. But alas, the financial problems of our conglomerate have spread to our door, and we are now faced with an enormous deficit. If that deficit is not soon made up, we may be forced to close the library, depriving hundreds of employees of a major resource.

TALK MONEY RIGHT OFF

> To keep the Company Library from closing, we need you to approve the enclosed authorization for an extra $100,000 above budget by June 1. Otherwise we'll have to sell off the contents in June. The reasons are . . .

Yes, when you get to the point quickly, it sounds aggressive, energetic, maybe even a bit feisty, but you're doing your readers a favor. You've made it clear what this pile of paper is about. That way they can see what the details relate to, as they read. (Or they can toss it away, and not have it take up any more of their time.) You've taken a stand. You've let them know what you think. That way they don't have to worm it out of you. Finally, you've shown them what you want them to do, making it easier for them to say "Sure!"

□ TALK ABOUT PEOPLE □

||||||||||||||||||||||||||||||||||||||||||||||||||||||||||||||||||||||||||

S trange beasts catch our attention quickly, but what really intrigues us is a human being.

The more words you have referring to people, the more people will like to read your work. Start with names—first names, if that's polite. Expand people's initials. Add descriptions that show relationship—"my boss," "his third cousin," "a close friend." Of course, these aren't essential to your argument, but they give us some feeling of human contact.

If you're reporting on a meeting or interview, think of it as a piece of drama. Look for moments of confrontation, conflict, the stuff of theater. You don't have to write the scene up as a soap opera, however, to show the reader glimpses of excitement. Just relate this material to your main point.

For instance, you could report a showdown over a contract this way:

DRAB—AND UNINFORMATIVE:

> We met with Townsend's representative, Thiebault, and presented our position. He informed us that he will be consulting with their lawyers.

MORE DRAMATIC—AND INFORMATIVE

We met Tom Thiebault, who started right out by saying, "I'm sure we can work this out."

Al read him our position paper. Tom sat there getting
whiter by the minute. At the end, he said, "I'm shocked.
I had no idea you were thinking this way."

Al said, "What are you going to do?"

Tom sighed, and seemed to stagger as he got up. "I
guess I'll have to talk with our lawyers. I still hope we can
work something out."

When you include observations like this, along with actual
quotes, you make it easier for the reader to draw intelligent
conclusions about the meeting. A touch of the novelistic can
help you convey the significant shadings, the implications of a
conversation, and these are often more revealing than the abstract summary.

Use direct quotations, too; they're more accurate, and they
help the reader get a feeling for the person speaking. Also, if
you ever have to protect yourself or build a case, those quotations make very convincing evidence.

Feel free to incorporate conversational elements into your
prose, in all but the most formal presentations (and there
are very few of those). That way, the readers can take your
writing as a talk, not a sermon. For instance, you could include:

- contractions, like *it's*, *can't*, *won't*. These make
  sense, and they are often more understandable than
  the longer forms;
- questions ("What do you think?");
- direct address ("John, I need your answer soon.");
- occasional repetitions ("The bank—yes, the bank—
  reported in on Tuesday with another offer.");
- sentence fragments, once in a while ("Like this.").

Along these lines, feel free to use the words *you*, *me,* and *I.* I know you may have been warned in high school never to use those words in your papers. They were too informal. But they make sense. When you mean you and me, say so.

You could also decide to let more of your own emotions show. This takes a decision. In the past, you may have learned to conceal "bad" emotions, such as anger, fear, guilt. And of course, you could make yourself look foolish, if you just got mad in your writing without showing why. So be sure to describe what led you to feel that way. If you do, you'll become a character in your own report, not just a bystander. You'll stir people up, sway them to your side. The more feelings you express, the more your "significance"—the meaning in your writing—grows. That's natural.

After all, as Goethe said, it's a natural impulse to want to communicate your own personality:

> What gives a person significance is not the accumulation he leaves behind, but rather the activity and zest that permeates his life, and passes itself on to others.

So put yourself in your writing. You're people, too.

MAKE IT ACTIVE □

||||||||||||||||||||||||||||||||||||||||||||||||||||||||||||||||||||||||||||||

Active verbs stretch, turn, bend, struggle. Where possible, rewrite sentences so the verb turns active. Passive verbs just announce states of being:

I am   we are
it was   it will be
they were   they have been

| it might have been | it would have been |
| it had been | they are being |

Learn to see any form of the verb *to be* as a danger sign, because in the passive world, no one does anything. No one takes responsibility. Things just happen.

PASSIVE:

> The plant has been shut down this week because the boiler is in need of repairs.

TRANSLATION:

> I shut the plant down this week because Joe forgot to drain the boiler, and now we're fixing it.

When you make sentences active, they become clearer. You can see who did what.

People who feel tentative, apologetic, embarrassed, or frightened tend to cover their tracks by putting everything into the passive. For instance, a woman writing a report felt guilty about criticizing a program. She wrote: "This is a self-defeating motivation program." True. And her anger showed, despite her passive sentence. But how much more she would have said if she'd used active verbs: "This motivation program does not motivate anyone—it discourages them."

Guilt loves the passive. For instance, many of us learned that saying anything directly sounded awfully aggressive, even hostile. So we came to soften everything by making it sound as if God did it, or thought it, not us. For instance:

PASSIVE:

> There is a general sequential aspect to the effective design of organizational units.

TRANSLATION:

You must design these units in sequence.

When you spot a passive construction and rewrite it as an active one, you do two things:

1. You make it clear that someone must do something. The sentence acquires a person or thing as the subject—not just some vague "There" or "It."
2. You also suggest an action—more interesting than a state of being.

But that means admitting what you did, what they did, what you want them to do next. Simply changing your verbs makes you more honest. Notice what happens in revision:

BEFORE:	AFTER:
It might be helpful if you did this . . .	Do this . . .
It is important for the reader to observe . . .	Observe . . .
You would be well advised to be aware of . . .	Notice . . .

Why did people use the passive here? Because they were afraid to give orders. But they were anyway, under the smokescreen of humble passives. So if you're telling someone to do something, tell them—actively.

Just this one change—making most of your passive verbs active—can give your style muscles.

☐ *LEAVE YOUR NOUNS ALONE* ☐

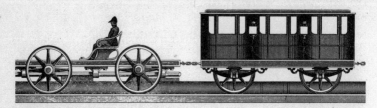

One reason people write badly is that they try to cram too much into one sentence, and in the process, they turn three or four perfectly good nouns or verbs into adjectives—a terrible fate. The result is ambiguity.

For instance, what does this mean?

> "Task orientation publication architecture" (from a computer company's manual)

Is it a building? Is it a series of publications? Is it an orientation seminar? Or is it a building to house books about job orientation? When you hook too many nouns together, you get a big train. Often you end up without an engine. If you sometimes compress your meaning into noun freight trains like this, take the time to uncouple them. You may have to use more words, even create new sentences, but you'll make more sense. For instance, what the writer above meant was:

> A way of designing a series of publications around the jobs that the readers actually do

Clearer, no?

Leave nouns alone. Let them do their work. Don't bend them into these awful trains, the way German does. When you try to make a noun act like an adjective, you risk confusion; the reader begins to wonder what modifies what, and how. Whenever you begin to rely too much on modifiers, and too little on the nouns themselves, vagueness creeps in.

How do these horrors accumulate? Well, for one thing, their writers treat words as if they were railroad cars, always loaded with the same freight. But words change their meaning as their context changes.

For instance, if you've explained a term like "product usability" and you're now talking about setting standards, you might write some chained-together phrase like "product usability standard setting." But when you spot that throat-choker, you should revise it to read, "setting standards to make sure our products are usable." But, to say that, you would have to pay attention to what you mean—not to rote phrases. Yes, people would have been able to parse the clunky phrase into its parts, and figure out its meaning. But why make them struggle just because you like to use shorthand?

Here's another example of the way these freight trains get started. A personnel director had spent a paragraph talking about job enrichment. He said it was a trend and an area of study. Finally getting to his point, he asked rhetorically, "What is happening on the job enrichment front?"

He probably thought that was a clever way to sum up what he'd been saying, but it's just clumsy. If he had noticed the awkwardness, he could have thought through his sentence again, and asked something like: "What new ideas have come out of our study of ways to enrich our jobs?"

Too simple? Yes, that's another reason for these concatenations, these linkings-together of nouns—false dignity. They sound like uninspired professors trying to impress each other. There's a certain academic odor to them, but little intelligence. So break down these noun clumps into their meanings.

Another important point: a strong verb generates the motive force behind a sentence. But what do some people do instead? They turn some poor noun into a makeshift verb, like this:

> Let's quality-circle this proposal. Let's solution this
> problem. Let's interface on this.

These noun-verbs just sound klutzy. They show lazy thinking and faddism.

One English sentence can magnificently express one idea. But sentences are built on nouns and verbs. If you transform a noun into something it's not—an adjective, say, or an ersatz verb—you risk diluting your meaning, suggesting several ideas, none clearly.

Go the other direction. When you find yourself spawning one of these noun clumps or noun-verbs, pause to translate. You'll end up with a sentence or two more. But at least you'll be writing English.

□ *USE ALL SIX SENSES* □

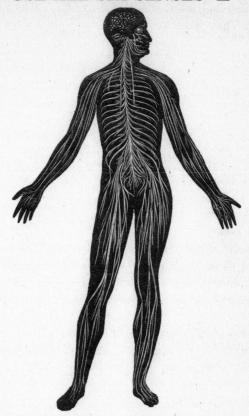

Y ou have five—no, six—senses. Use them all when you write.

Most writing sounds as if the writer only had a brain. No hands. No eyes. No nose or ears. We get few textures, colors, sounds, smells, tastes. These may be incidental, but they help us understand whatever you're talking about—envision the actual meeting, imagine the real product.

Replace the abstract with the specific:

ABSTRACT:	SPECIFIC:
We provide high-technology accuracy.	We make sure the read-write head goes in exactly the right place.
A floppy.	A disk that looks like a slightly limp 45-rpm record tucked into a 5¼" square black jacket.
A human-engineered keyboard.	A keyboard designed to meet your fingertips, with keys that have just enough "give."

In your mind's eye, replay the scene. Ask yourself questions: how does it feel? Rough? Smooth? Soft? Hard? Heavy? Light? Does it have a distinctive smell or taste? How big is it? What color? What shape and design? What sounds does it make?

By reporting on what you notice, you help the readers to get a feeling for your experience. You put them in your place.

That's where your sixth sense comes in. Use your intuition to figure out what the reader might be wondering about from moment to moment. What half-formed questions are arising? What longings, worries, curiosities? As you write, pay attention to these hunches. If you think a reader may have a question, answer it—concretely. If a worry, admit that some people might get frightened at this point, and say why. What looks odd, sounds funny, smells strange?

In this way, you show you're following the readers' reactions. That's reassuring. It helps keep their attention. And because you answer their questions as you go, you keep the subject clear.

For instance, in writing about a new machine to be tested by a customer, you might say:

Of course, at this point, you may get worried, because the red lights flash at the top of the panel, and the gears make a grinding noise, as if they couldn't quite mesh. But that's normal. They are in what we call syncro-mesh, an oiled glide into position.

In about ten seconds, the red lights go out, and the axle begins to turn again. You may smell a slight trace of oil at this point. Don't worry. It's just given off by the hot parts. You can make sure the oil level is okay by looking at the gauge on the bottom right of your screen.

Such specifics are not always appropriate. Sometimes you can give the details the first time you mention a subject, then use the abstract term from then on. Sometimes you're talking as one expert to another, and you don't want to sound insultingly simple. Or you're just dashing off a confirming memo. But most readers appreciate specifics. Take a look at any popular magazine. Its paragraphs blossom with light, sound, air.

Actually, most writers omit specifics because they're lazy. It's hard enough to notice specific items, much less to record these observations. One relatively painless way to learn is to keep a notebook. Watch your muscles clench during meetings. When does your jaw get tight? Whose voice seems to make your calves and feet contract? When do you hold your breath?

Remember yourself. Deep inside, you have an observer, a constant neutral witness to your posture, gesture, facial expression, breathing, taste, impressions of light and sound. Don't leap to interpret. Just be there and observe.

By synthesizing all this news coming from your nerves, your intuition grows quicker and stronger. You could say that your intuition perceives in a different way—faster, surer, more comprehensive—than reason ever could.

So go beyond logic. Listen to all six senses, and write down what they say.

□ *PUT IT IN NUMBERS* □

H ow many people worked aboard this nineteenth-century French ship? I see eighty-three. But someone must have gone aloft. And anyway, this is just a picture.

We yearn for facts. What's the exact count? Is that an average? Do we have proof?

Numbers impress us. They seem precise, inarguable, convincing. Managers rely on numbers as a final test of productivity, profit, results. Numbers give the reader a way to measure how important the subject is, no matter what you say. They show you've done your homework. You're not just talking through your hat.

So take the time to work up figures, particularly for key parts of your argument—the parts that someone else might dispute. And as you write, revise from the general to the numeric:

VAGUE:

Recently, we have seen a gradual increase.
Dozens of people came in the first day.
You'll face a fairly high rate here.

NUMERIC:

We have seen a 20% gain each year for the last five years.

114 people came in the first day.
You'll face a 50% earned-income rate.

Don't machine-gun us with statistics, though. Too many numbers in a paragraph, and many people skip to the next page. So ask yourself: do I really need this?

Help us see the meaning of these numbers. Use diagrams, charts, graphs. Print your tables large enough for us to read. And cushion the numbers with interpretation. Raw data means little, even to an expert. Explain what the numbers mean. If you show a table, point out the important parts in a caption and in the text. Don't force me to figure it out by myself.

Prepare me for complex sets of data. Tell me what I'm going to find. Then afterward, make sure I see how it ties into your main argument. For instance:

We see a clear movement toward increasing shelf space for doughnuts, no matter what size the store.

ANNUAL GROSS	HAVE DECREASED	INCREASED	SAME	NO ANSWER
$200,000	18%	58%	15%	9%
$500,000	5%	71%	12%	12%
$1,000,000	4%	75%	12%	9%
$2,000,000	16%	59%	14%	11%

You can see that stores in the middle range (half a million to around a million a year) have increased shelf space for doughnuts even more than the top-volume and low-volume stores. That's another reason we urge concentrating on these middle-range markets.

Whenever you face statistics that make your case look bad, admit it. That way you can give your excuses. You may not defuse the reader's doubt, but you can at least show you're being honest. Don't leave it to the readers to do some quick penciling, and note that you've left out a key fact, or glossed it over. That really looks bad.

Also, don't exaggerate. Don't say "thousands" when, at best, it was 999. Round off conservatively. When you're reviewing your draft, go through it once just checking your figures.

And play fair. You may have read Darrell Huff's wonderful book, *How to Lie with Statistics*. But resist the temptation to confuse average, median, and mean. If you've run a survey, say how many people you sampled, out of how large a population, and what your percentage of error is. If figures aren't really relevant, don't use them—even if you're writing a TV commercial.

☐ *KEEP IT SHORT* ☐

||||||||||||||||||||||||||||||||||||||||||||||||||||||||||||||||||||||||||||||||||||||||||||||||||||

This is what too many reports end up looking like: extra comments piled on top of unnecessary sections, surrounded with useless appendices, decorated with flourishes, monuments, and filigree work. At the center, a catafalque for any idea the writer may have started with. Inside that, a coffin.

This over-decoration buries your meaning. So, if you're not

making sets for an eighteenth-century opera, keep it short.
Pare away the extras.

Short words, short sentences, short paragraphs. Why?

- They're easy to digest.
- I can see what it's about, fast.
- I don't get cross-eyed looking at the page.
- I get frequent breaks, between the blocks of prose.

So, despite what you may have learned in school and the military, choose the small word over the big one as you write. Sometimes, of course, you must use the twenty-eight-letter term because it's the only accurate word. But when you do find two words that mean the same thing, prefer the shorter one. For instance,

REPLACE THIS:	WITH THIS:
Activate	Start
Implement	Run
Initiate	Start
Modification	Change
Preparatory to	Before
Re-initialize	Start over
Utilize	Use

Reduce phrases, too.

REPLACE THIS:	WITH THIS:
At this point in time	Now
Due to the fact that	Because
Exhibits a tendency	Tends
I am of the opinion that	I think
In a certain number of instances	Sometimes
You will find enclosed	Here is

If you do this, your sentences will tighten up, too. Long sentences are hard to follow. Most people can remember seven or eight words at a stretch. After that, they begin to lose track. Compare these two sentences:

46 WORDS:

> For the product we have just been discussing, our reported sales figures show a definite decline in the number of units being sold, but on the other hand our profit-and-loss sheets also can be examined to indicate an equally definite uptick in dollar volume.

7 WORDS:

> We sold fewer units, made more dollars.

Which is easier to grasp? Has any meaning been lost?

I'm not recommending that you make every sentence seven words long. You'd sound like a robot—choppy and not too bright. Vary the length of your sentences according to their meanings. But trim every one. That way, when you need to make a point, you can emphasize it by drawing up short. Get it?

"Every word you add dilutes the sentence," says the contemporary American poet Miller Williams. In fact, whenever you throw in a significant qualification, you risk distracting the reader from the main idea. So watch out for sentences that:

- Combine three or four ideas. Sort them out into three or four sentences.
- Have more than one adverbial clause (beginning with *when*, *because*, *although*, *whereas*, *after,* and *before*). A hint that one should start another sentence.
- Contain more than one *that*, *which*, or *who* clause. Who's who? Which which is that? Again, a sign to turn one sentence into two or three.
- Take up more than three regular lines of text.

Look at the length of your paragraphs, too. Few things repel readers more than paragraphs that take up three-quarters of a page. Leave that to novelists like William Faulkner.

To trim a paragraph, you can:

- Make sure you've got events in order. This may cut your paragraph in half, if you've been jumping forward and doubling back.
- Ax sentences that repeat the same information, with some minor variation or flourish.
- Leave out redundant examples.
- Throw out anything that does not focus on the central idea of this paragraph.

Here's an example:

ORIGINAL:

Our study showed that potential customers preferred even U.S. savings bonds to stocks. For instance, some would rather put their money in life insurance. Others preferred to refinance their mortgages. Some just put their money in savings accounts. Remember that in our survey we asked people what they would do with $10,000 extra cash. We found stocks came in ninth, after other types of investment. Another way to put this is that our brokers face a difficult job persuading people to shift funds out of these other types of investment, into stocks. Of course, we may need to hire a different breed of broker. But that's another kettle of fish. The really important thing to keep in mind here is that we have a hard row to hoe before we'll get people to invest in stocks.

REVISION:

When we asked potential customers what they would do with $10,000 extra cash, they said they'd put it in eight types of investment—including life insurance and U.S. Savings Bonds—before they bought stocks. So our brokers face a difficult job of persuasion.

A paragraph ought to express an idea—one idea. The sentences inside offer refinements, details, evidence. If they don't support that idea, they're in the wrong paragraph.

In some ways writing resembles carpentry. The longer most carpenters work, the more they love simple forms. When the Italian designer Giuseppe Galli Bibiena showed an old carpenter the design for the elaborate monument in the picture at the beginning of this chapter, the carpenter asked, "Is it a cake or a tomb?"

□ *CUT OUT JARGON AND CLICHÉS* □

J argon and in-house clichés resemble tonsils—organs that have outlived their usefulness. Chop them out. You know how someone else's gobbledygook puts you off. When you run into too much jargon you may feel stupid (This authority knows everything and you can't figure out one word). Or put down (This authority only talks to other authorities. The rest of us should feel lucky to listen in). Or angry (You want to understand something, but the writer won't help you). Or afraid. (You may figure that if you can't follow this stuff, you'll never be able to handle this part of your job).

Inside the shop, we use abbreviations (*IV* for *intravenous*), acronyms (ICU for *Intensive Care Unit*, GOMER for *Get Out*

Of My Emergency Room) to talk faster. We create and use special terms, which describe only one or two objects, to avoid the ambiguity of ordinary language, in which one word may have half a dozen meanings, none of them too specific. And in some in-house memos, these shorthand forms say a lot in a short space.

If we're worried that someone else may not recognize us as expert in the field, though, we may show off with a lot of jargon. After a while, we may even feel unprofessional if we don't rely on insider's terms.

But even experts don't need to read jargon all the time. You can help them out by replacing most of it with ordinary terms—except when the jargon's more specific.

And these esoteric terms tend to overwhelm outsiders. The same phrase that means so much to you has no meaning at all for someone who's new to the field.

So before you reach for a technical term, ask yourself: do I really need this? Couldn't I say the same thing just as accurately if I chose an ordinary term? Often you can.

But what if you use jargon without knowing it? That's common. You've been in the same business for a few years, you've learned the lingo now, and when you use those terms inside your group, many people know what you mean. But not outside your department or company. That's where you begin to get puzzled reactions.

If that sounds familiar, you might start making up a list of all the technical terms you use:

- Review everything you write, pulling out the shoptalk.
- Next to each term, put a valid substitute—a phrase that an ordinary reader would understand. (Note when you may and may not use the substitute.)
- Collect lists of these terms from trade magazines, and handbooks. Put the ones you yourself use on your own list.

- If you use a spelling checker on your word processor, delete these from your main dictionary, so they will be highlighted. Since they won't be in the dictionary, your system will suspect that these are misspellings, and point them out to you.

Also, be consistent. A newcomer to computers might think there was a significant difference between *boot* and *start*. There isn't. But if you use now one term, now the other, a reader may begin looking for some differences in meaning. That way lies chaos.

You could set yourself some standards. On your list, make a note to yourself to use *x*, not *z*. For instance, there may be three perfectly good words that describe the machine you sell. Pick one word and stick to it. The first time you use a word you know will be unfamiliar to readers, define it. From then on, where necessary, use the definition rather than, or in addition to the term. For instance, when you first use the word *byte*, you might define it this way:

That takes one byte. A byte is eight bits.

But what are bits?

Maybe you've already defined those, eight pages earlier. But that's a long time ago. Who could remember? So expand your definition, like this:

That takes one byte. A byte is eight bits (the on or off signals, positive or negative charges that make sense to the computer). That's enough to code one of the 128 symbols we use—letters, numbers, special command characters, and punctuation. Essentially, one byte equals one letter.

Pause when the new term comes up. Take the time to explain. You don't speed people up by confusing them. You just make them go back and go back and go back, to decipher your cryptic comments.

Also, create a glossary. That's a compendium of key terms, with definitions, in the back of your report. That way, if readers forget what a term means, they can look it up in the back, rather than thumbing through all the pages, trying to find that paragraph where you first mentioned it.

Beware of applying these terms to nontechnical subjects. That sounds odd and often a little too cute. For instance,

TOO CUTE:	*WRITE THIS INSTEAD:*
Let's boot this plan.	Let's put this plan in motion.
I'll byte.	I'm interested.
Let's debug the human interface problems.	Let's resolve this feud.

You can be precise without most jargon. So cut it out.

□ *ELIMINATE BIAS* □

Do you think of your employees as a bunch of clowns? If you do, don't bother with this chapter. If you think better of your co-workers—and your readers—you'll want to eliminate unconscious bias from your writing.

I'm sure you're not prejudiced against other ethnic, racial, and age groups, against people of the opposite sex or of another sexual persuasion, against handicapped folks—or not much. But you may still talk as if you are. Or you may still be using phrases that have come to seem "prejudiced" to some audiences, even though you don't mean anything particularly nasty by them.

Unconsciously biased writing can hurt and enrage some

readers; when they feel bruised and mad, they won't listen to anything else you have to say. Worse, you may subtly encourage other people in your organization to act on their worst prejudices. Biased writing is always undemocratic, usually illegal, often stupid, self-destructive, and unprofitable. Here's how to stop it.

Keep in mind that your language indicates—and limits—what you think. Many traditional phrases come from stereotypes held by people in Northern Europe hundreds of years ago. Some come from yesterday's TV. The language of our culture encourages us to talk in ways that discriminate. So beware of phrases that come a bit too easily.

Make sure that you don't somehow assume that everyone in a particular group acts in the same way. For example, if you have to write about retirees, do you generally picture them as doddering and senile? Are all women emotional, unaggressive, bad at math? Are all gay men sissies, all handicapped people vegetables?

You'd never say those things directly. But some of what you say may still imply that you do think that way. For instance, you might be surprised that an accountant turned out to be a woman. Would you be inclined to say "a woman accountant" when you'd never think of calling a man "a male accountant"? Such distinctions discriminate.

So drop all indications of what group someone belongs to. In most cases, your reader has no need to know that so-and-so is part Sioux, part Norwegian. Is it really necessary to say, "He is an old black man"? Such descriptions imply that most people aren't—or at least, most people in your company aren't.

You probably wouldn't use slurs like *honkey*, *pussywhipped*, *dumb lunk*, *pervert*, and *cripple*. But you might accidentally slip into a phrase that is emotionally charged for some group, because the words could refer to their color, gender, age, or physical ability. For example:

Free, white, and twenty-one
A Chinaman's chance
He had a yellow streak
Lily white
White as snow
Straight as the day is long
Gay old time
Thinks like a man
That time of the month
Play the tough guy
A program with balls

You might reread your manuscript once, just looking for phrases that could be misconstrued as a subtle putdown of some group.

In those rare cases when you actually have to describe a particular group, as when you report on progress in affirmative action, use the government's terms. (These change every few years.) Currently, *minority* is an okay term. Definitely out: phrases like "our nonwhite employees" or "culturally disadvantaged applicants." Those imply that white is right and that some applicants have no culture. Beware, too, of suggesting that middle-age white heterosexual males are all that count. Translate

FROM THIS:	*TO THIS:*
Mankind	People, or human beings
Manmade	Synthetic
Manpower	Workforce
Straight with us	Honest with us
That's white of you	That's generous

Don't use *he* as a general term for *everyone*. If you're faced with a sentence that begins like this, "When the employee reports, he . . ." rewrite by:

1. Cutting out the *he*:   When reporting, the employee . . .
2. Changing to plural: When the employees report, they . . .
3. Using *you:*   When you report, . . .
4. Using *he/she*   When the employee reports, he or she . . .

(That last one, the *h/she*, *he/she*, *he-or-she* mishmash, smells of bureaucratic precision. Avoid it when you can.)

Avoid unnecessary distinctions. For instance, why tell us who's married and unmarried in a business letter? And particularly, why tell us that about women, but not men? Call women Ms., not Mrs. or Miss. And if you use first and last names for one sex, use them for all.

NOT:	*INSTEAD:*
Mr. Ronald Pevsner and Janet introduced the new product.	Mr. Ronald Pevsner and Ms. Janet Hogie introduced the new product.

Revise job titles too.

NOT:	*INSTEAD:*
Policeman	Police officer
Foreman	Supervisor
Chairman	Chairperson

And don't single out rare birds. For instance, when you say that Joe is the first male secretary in the department, you show you think it's unusual. That may be true, but is that the point you're making? If so, include the detail. Otherwise, cut it out. The same goes for supposedly encouraging phrases like "our first female forklift driver" and "our first Hispanic vice-president."

Taking the time and effort to revise expressions like these can make even an even-tempered writer snort and rumple the page. After all, you're changing your habits. But if you persevere, you'll find that in time you no longer have to worry about sounding prejudiced. Who knows? You might uncover and cleanse some remaining stains of bias.

☐ *SAY NO—BUT DON'T MAKE*
AN ENEMY ☐

In 1892, when the iron workers in Homestead, Pennsylvania, asked for a raise, Andrew Carnegie sent a one-word telegram from Europe: "No." 3,000 workers went out on strike and Carnegie responded with armed Pinkertons, who killed two dozen people. Then the crowd seized several Pinkertons and ran them through this gauntlet. That night, local hospitals treated more than two hundred people for gunshot and stab wounds, burns, gougings, and near-drownings.

The sheriff knew better than to get involved. And if you don't want to get caught up in a violent argument, watch how you say no.

When you say no in person, you can qualify it with kind looks, friendly gestures, sympathetic tones. But when you're writing, you've only got words to work with. You may be tempted to rely on canned phrases and brush off the reader in a few "fishy" paragraphs, to take back everything you said, or to make a dozen excuses for your position.

The problem is that a rejection letter in this style sounds so insincere that it drives readers crazy. They can hear the falsity, guilt, and contempt. You've turned a "no" into a lost customer.

If you really feel bad about a decision, maybe you should change the decision. That's cleaner than writing a weasel-worded apology. But if the basic decision makes sense, make it clear. Don't start off by sounding apologetic. Too many apologies, and the reader will think you're willing to take it all back. You invite new letters, proposals, desperate phone calls. You reopen what you've decided to close.

Tone is the hardest part of saying no. If you're mad, you may be tempted to let loose and write things like, "That's the most idiotic damn complaint I ever heard." Then, drawing back, you might revise that to bureaucratese: "Current company policies do not permit the accession to your request." The best tactic is to show some compassion.

You could start by talking about the reader. Find some point you have in common, something you both agree on. Show that you understand the reader's position. For instance, you could start your letter in this way:

- You're perfectly right to be disturbed at the damaged parts.
- You have spotted a problem our company ought to pay more attention to.
- I can understand how upset you must have been.

You can afford some praise, perhaps a small concession.

Then say no. And say it straight. Here again, tone can distort your meaning. If you're too blunt, you'll sound angry, rude, even hostile. To avoid that, many people hide their meaning in a tangle of qualifications. Just say no neutrally.

TOO BLUNT:

You'll never work here.

TOO TANGLED:

Taking into account our current hiring posture and the job specifications of the position for which your application appears to be submitted, I'm afraid that our current policies prohibit me from extending an offer of employment to you, although this is, of course, no reflection on your abilities and hirability.

NEUTRAL:

I'm sorry, but we don't have a job for you.

Give some explanation, too, but make it convincing. Not "It's against company policy"—that says nothing. And don't give some false reason, either: you're just inviting arguments, lawsuits, further letters.

Don't add too much reasoning, either, unless you have to persuade the reader to accept the turndown. (Then you're really facing a sales job.) Just provide one or two real reasons, stated in a few sentences each.

There are a lot of times you won't want to tell the truth about the reasons. It might sound too insulting. ("Your résumé was covered with a gray sticky substance. So we threw it out.") Or too embarrassing to you. ("You were well qualified for this job, but the boss's nephew got it.")

In these cases, you still need to give some explanation, without resorting to meaningless phrases. At least state the facts. For instance, you could add something like this:

- We've hired someone else.
- Your plan cost too much.
- As we see it, you are responsible for the damages.

Then suggest something else they can do next. If possible, give details. For instance, if you think the applicant has a chance at some other company, give the name of the person responsible for hiring. Or, if you won't fix their machine, name someone who might.

Wish them well, if you can stand it. You could cuss them out. But if you think there's a chance they could still like you or your company, make an effort to be friendly. Again, watch out for the routine "best wishes." Think about it. Do you really wish this person well? If so, say how.

Most rejection letters take less than a page. If you want to show you've really looked over their case, take more time. Give them extra information, even if it's not too relevant. Tell them what your company plans to do in the next year, what changes you're making, what type of competition they faced. Say what kind of business you want to do with them in the future.

Just don't start an argument. If you think you've written a letter that will provoke anger or hope, put it away for a day or two. If you still want to send it, ask friends or colleagues what they think.

During the Civil War, Abraham Lincoln wrote a lot of furious messages to his headstrong generals, but he put these pages on top of his desk, and never mailed them. The next day he usually wrote—and dispatched—more carefully reasoned letters. When General Joseph Hooker got one of these, he began to cry, saying:

That is just such a letter as a father might write to his son. It is a beautiful letter, and although I think he was harder on me than I deserved, I will say that I love the man that wrote it.

You don't have to make an enemy, then. Just say no with compassion.

□ *LOOSEN UP YOUR LAYOUT* □

||||||||||||||||||||||||||||||||||||||||||||||||||||||||||||||||||||||||||||||||||||||||||||

Some reports look like a lot of words crowded into a small space. Black text from side to side, top to bottom. No light, no air.

Opening up your layout can give readers some fresh air, so they can look down on your report as if from the top of the Parachute Jump at Coney Island. They can see how all the parts fit together. They can decide for themselves what to read and what to skip. You show them what's important, what's not.

You start with white space. Leave some around whatever you write. For instance, make all your margins at least an inch and a half wide. Just doing that will give your readers the feeling that they have plenty of time and room. Already, you've made your report look like a lot less work to read.

Next, put in some headlines. They break up the text and highlight your key ideas, so people can come back to them later, without hunting all night for them. A strong heading expresses what the reader thinks and wants—not what you and your company believe. For instance:

AVOID:	*INSTEAD:*
Accessorization	Adding Components to Your Copier
Bells and Whistles	Those Little Extras
Sophisticated Diagnostics	How to Tell What's Wrong

Sum up what's interesting—to the reader—about the next few paragraphs. Use verbs to show actions. For instance:

AVOID:	*INSTEAD:*
The Bottom Line	What It All Adds Up to
Problem Solution Tables	Solving Problems
Video Camera Operation	Using Your Video Camera

If you want to show that one section is less important than another, and another one even less important, you can give each heading different weight. For instance:

HOW TO MAKE SOMETHING LOOK VERY IMPORTANT

How to Make Something Look a Little Less Important

HOW TO SHOW THIS IS MUCH LESS IMPORTANT

If you're going to have a series of headings, make them consistent and sequential. For instance, if the first one ends in *-ing*, make the rest in that series end in *-ing*. Arrange sections in order, and show that order in something more than the numbering system.

AVOID:	*INSTEAD:*
Tabulating the Results	Who We Talked to
Who Was Surveyed	What We Asked
Preliminary Impressions	What We Thought at First
The Questionnaire	How It All Adds Up

Another way you can open up your layout is to take any list you've got and break it out. Take it out of the paragraph and display it as a bulleted list. (Bullets can be done as asterisks, or dashes, or elevated periods.) If the list has been arranged in a 1–2–3 sequence, use numbers. Here are examples.

— Residential
— Commercial
— Industrial

Or:

• Operating process
• Real output
• Benchmarks

Or:

1. Preparing remittance advices
2. Comparing cash-receipts totals
3. Reconciling

And include some pictures, too: cartoons for entertainment, diagrams, drawings, flow charts, organization charts— anything that condenses text into an image. That will help readers who don't like reading as much as you like writing.

Yes, and business graphics, too. (See the next chapter.)

Use your looser layout, then, to give your readers more choices:

- to read it all, or just parts—or none of it;
- to stop reading for a while, to look at pictures;
- to come back later, and find information fast, in a heading, diagram, or list;
- to skim through a list to find the one item they want;
- to take an occasional break.

□ *ADD BUSINESS GRAPHICS* □

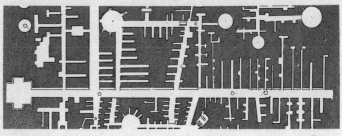

A chart is a map through a maze of numbers. Without that map, your readers may bump into walls in the dark, get lost in catacombs, drop into pits.

Most reports show us messy circles, squiggly bar-and-column graphs, dimly shaded area charts. Even when a computer has made them, the reasoning gets obscured under too many lines and too few labels. Yet the whole point of using graphics is to make the numbers clear.

Well-done graphics can show off your precision, speed, and honesty. They help people who think visually, not verbally. They often communicate much more than a page of text, particularly when you are describing trends, contrasts, comparisons, measurable relationships, the flow of a process.

Not sure that charts apply? If you are writing about any of the standard business and accounting topics, you can liven up your presentation by adding sharp business graphics. But you have to pick the kind of chart that will make your point. Try a few different approaches before settling on a particular format. For instance, if you wanted to show sales figures for seven products over the last two years, you might start by trying to fit those into a pie chart, on the assumption that these seven products represented your full output. Your result might look like this:

1982 SALES: $1,114,500

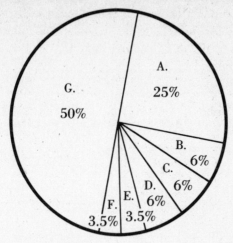

1983 SALES $3,123,000

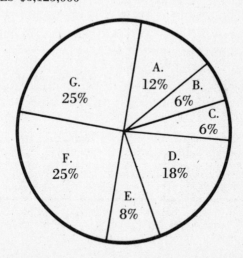

LEGEND

A = Health Pack   E = Lower Back Pack
B = Life Extension Pack F = Headache Pack
C = Yoga Pack   G = Herbal Pack
D = Foot Pack

Those two pie charts show a lot about the relative importance of the products, from one year to the next. But they don't make it easy for the reader to see how many dollars more or less a product sold in 1983 than in 1982. For that, you need vertical columns, like this:

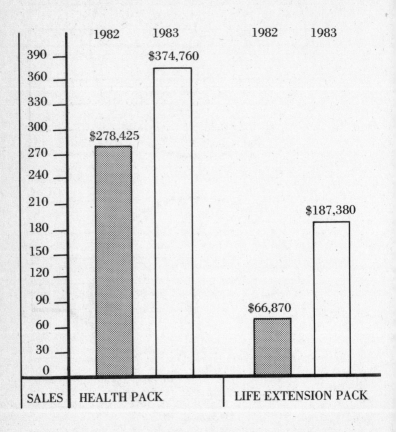

So experiment a bit before deciding what kind of chart you're going to make. Then test out your chart on someone.

Make key lines or points stand out, too. The grid's not as important as the data.

NOT THIS:

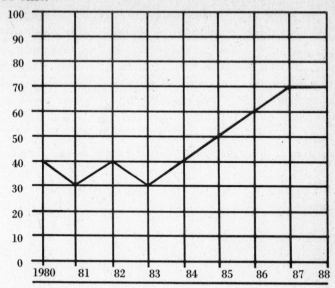

BUT THIS:

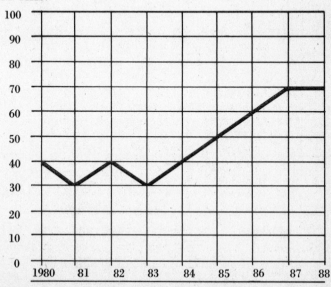

Use a heavy hand on the meaningful material, then. Leave the other stuff in the background.

If you're shading in some areas, do the shading in some recognizable progression, not higgledy-piggledy. For instance, go from white boxes through gray to black; from thin lines to thick; from red to orange to yellow. (Don't strive for unusual cross-hatchings. They become interesting in themselves, deflecting the reader from the point.) And don't forget to include a legend explaining what each type of shading means. If you have enough space put the labels right in the middle, like this:

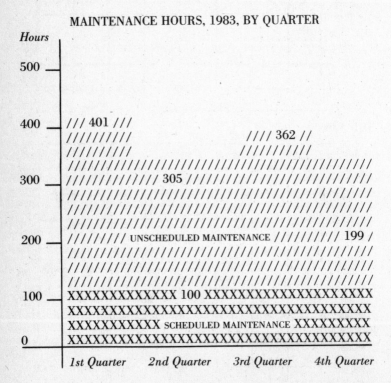

MAINTENANCE HOURS, 1983, BY QUARTER

LEGEND: /// = UNSCHEDULED MAINTENANCE
XXX = SCHEDULED MAINTENANCE

Notice that this chart could also include a dotted line showing the average hours spent on maintenance that year. But that extra information belongs on the next chart. Too many lines, too many areas, and you stupefy the viewer.

In general, make more graphs—in sequence—rather than crowding a lot of elements onto one. Include two or three elements per graph, and certainly not more than five.

For instance, you could have a pie chart with thirty slices, but most people would find that confusing. Instead, group some of those slices together in categories when you show us the material the first time. For instance, you could summarize the results of your study of who does what in your company in this fashion:

WHO DOES WHAT

(Percentage of Our Employees in Major Job Groups)

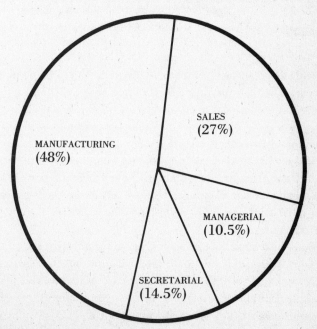

Then split up each category, like this:

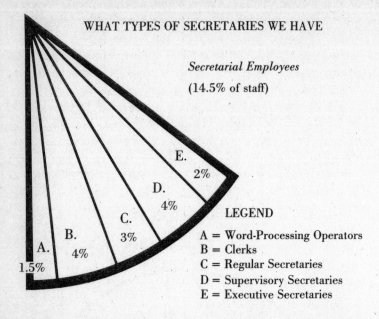

WHAT TYPES OF SECRETARIES WE HAVE

Secretarial Employees
(14.5% of staff)

E.
2%

D.
4%

C.
3%

B.
4%

A.
1.5%

LEGEND
A = Word-Processing Operators
B = Clerks
C = Regular Secretaries
D = Supervisory Secretaries
E = Executive Secretaries

Only when you've briefed readers on the details can you risk showing them all the little slices in one big pie. Then they can make some sense out of those slivers. So in general, figure out which interrelationships are most important, and do graphs for each one, rather than lumping them all together.

Make your labels easy to read, too. Don't arrange them vertically, for instance. Why should I have to tilt the page to find out what that axis signifies? Don't make them tiny, either. If you have a lot of qualifications, put those in a caption at the bottom.

Be honest about the zero level as well. To distort the growth of sales, you could show only the grid from 500 to 550, so an increase from $500 to $530 would look dramatic. But play it straight. Put in the rest of the grid—even though the real increase in sales is not so spectacular after all.

SPECTACULAR INCREASE IN SALES !!!

Dollars Per Year

	(1980)	(1982)	(1983)
$550,000			
$540,000			
$530,000			*
$520,000		*	
$510,000			
$500,000	*		
Year:	(1980)	(1982)	(1983)

SLOW GROWTH IN SALES

Dollars Per Year

(thousands)			
550			
540			
530			*
520		*	
510			
500	*		
490			
480			
470	(1980)	(1982)	(1983)
460			
450			
440			
430			
420			
410			
400			
390			
380			
370			
360			
350			
340			
330			
320			
310			
300			
290			
280			

270			
260			
250			
240			
230			
220			
210			
200			
190			
180			
170			
160			
150			
140			
130			
120			
110			
100			
90			
80			
70			
60			
50			
40			
30			
20			
10			
0			

If that looks too silly, arrange your graph so you show only the figures for the top hundred or so, then a jagged "tear," then the zero below, so we know you are omitting a lot. And add a caption with the percentage growth—that's the figure any interested reader will want to know.

SLOW GROWTH IN SALES

Dollars Per Year

(thousands)	(1980)	(1982)	(1983)
550			
540			
530			*
520		*	
510			
500	*		
490			
480			
470	(1980)	(1982)	(1983)
460			
450			
440			
430			
420			
410			
400			
. . . .			
. . . .			
30			
20			
10			
0			

This represents a 4% growth from 1980 to 1981, a little less than 2% from 1981 to 1982. Not too impressive.

Adding comments in your caption helps the reader interpret the data and relate it to the argument in your text.

If you've got the tools—a six-color printer, say, a plotter, or colored pens—fill in your charts with color. Anything other than black and white will brighten up the page. And people distinguish colors much faster than shapes. Look at the charts in any popular magazine. Cheerful, aren't they? (No matter what they mean.)

Instead of labels, the magazines tend to put in icons—representative images. Pigs, if the chart shows hog belly futures. Houses, if the chart shows housing starts. By all means, decorate if you can. Even a simple line drawing makes your chart into a picture.

When you're doing a flow chart, your boxes act as icons, indicating that we're now looking at a decision point, or some product kicked out by the system, or some information coming in. Make these large enough so we can read what's inside. Even if you're sure your readers are familiar with your symbols, provide a legend explaining what each shape means. Label your arrows, too, so we know why the procedure then moves from one box to the next, as shown on the following page:

CHECK-IN PROCEDURES

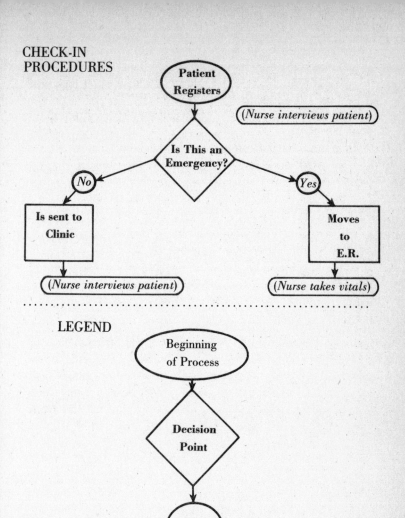

Patient Registers

(Nurse interviews patient)

Is This an Emergency?

No

Yes

Is sent to Clinic

Moves to E.R.

(Nurse interviews patient)

(Nurse takes vitals)

LEGEND

Beginning of Process

Decision Point

Answer

Physical Action

Leads to solution

Some people like to set charts off in boxes, others hate it. Whatever you use to distinguish your chart from text, be consistent. (Otherwise, readers will try to read some meaning into your lapses.)

In general, charts require just as much patience to prepare as text. After the hours you've spent finding the figures, preparing the calculations, choosing the right format, you may feel that making the chart should not take up much more of your time. You may not want to spend the extra time to put in labels, legends, titles, captions, and pictures. You may not be excited by the prospect of highlighting key lines, arranging shades and colors in some order, or eliminating distracting details. But if you don't, you're forcing your readers to spend valuable time puzzling over your meaning. And many won't bother.

□ *SUMMARIZE—AND STOP* □

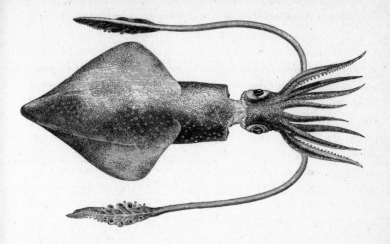

Some reports end with a squirt of ink, as half a dozen subjects float in the murk like tentacles ready to catch and strangle the unwary reader. No one knows what the point of the report is, and everyone feels free to swim away ignoring the whole mess.

For instance, some careless writers, at the end of a report:

- Take it all back. Just as you thought you had figured out what they meant, they say that perhaps they were incorrect, and maybe further research is needed. (A sign of cowardice. They got worried that someone might disagree.)

- Sum up what everyone else thinks—but omit their personal opinion. You want to know what they think, but you get pabulum.

- Ramble off into the distance. They sketch a hypotheti-

cal future in such detail that you forget what you're supposed to do tomorrow.
- End up discussing an unimportant side issue. They provide no summary of the main point, just a fade-out.

Sum up at the end. Give readers a capsulization to take away with them—not a laborious rehash of details, but a digest of your main point. And make sure that your readers know what you expect them to do next.

By the time you're writing the end of your report, you should know what you think. After all, you've written enough about your subject. Now look back over what you've done, and think:

- When people sum up my ideas, what do I want them to say? (If you wrote it effectively, they'll quote you without attribution, as if they'd thought of that way of expressing the idea.)
- What's the one idea I must get across? (One sentence, or at most one paragraph should be sufficient.)
- What do I want my readers to do now? (Something definite, measurable, by a certain deadline. Not just "think about this important subject"; rather, "Order the T100 by Tuesday, January 13th.")

Set your summary off from the rest of the text, so readers can flip back to it easily, days later, when they want to refresh their memory. Devote a separate section with a heading to it.

Once you've written your summary, revise your introduction so it points in the same direction. Often it will still reflect the ideas you started with—which may have changed as you wrote, and learned more.

Then stop. Once you've summed up what you think and what you want the reader to do, exit. Any more talk and you dilute your meaning, soften the urgency of your request.

After a real conclusion, silence speaks loudest.

□ *REVISE, REVISE* □

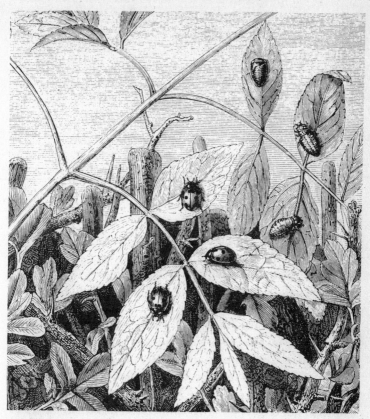

Most of us enjoy getting plants started. But who wants to weed, and pick off bugs, and fertilize, and transplant? That's what revising is like. You're cleaning up your prose, straightening out your organization, eliminating tangles and weak spots. Suddenly you're a critic, not a writer. That change can be confusing.

Leave yourself some time between writing and revising. Let the report cool off. That will help you get some distance from it, so you can look at it as if you were reading someone else's work.

Don't plunge into fine-tuning. If you start going through your document word by word, you can get lost in the details. I've known people who rewrote and rewrote and rewrote, and the results kept getting worse, because they were splicing together pieces of baling wire that held together hunks that didn't belong there.

Do what professional writers do: start with the larger issues of organization. That's more efficient because every change of order affects many, many more phrases. If you can rearrange sections so one flows naturally into the next, you'll find the writing clears up of its own accord.

Make several passes through your document, maintaining a neutral, not critical, mood. Don't browbeat yourself. Don't imagine yourself as a hostile reader, eager to spot flaws. Just read it as an interested student.

On the first reading, take notes on the organization, creating a rough outline of your sections. Then scrutinize that outline. Are the sections in a reasonable order, such as cause and effect; first, second, third, in order of time, size, or importance; main point, then evidence; or problem, analysis, solution?

Now it's time to shuffle sections around. If you found they were now in some accidental or nonsensical order, you may also have noticed that you've had to write some pretty tricky prose to explain why one section comes after another. So reorganizing can help you straighten out your sentences. Once you have developed an effective organization, you can write simply. (Of course, it helps to develop a solid structure *before* you write.)

Next, reread your work, paying attention to a slightly lower level of organization, following the argument carefully, to see if there are gaps or goofs. For instance, ask yourself:

- What should I add?
  Have I left out statistics that belong here? (Sometimes

you don't have them, but now you see you've got to dig them up.) Have I omitted some key step? (Look closely at all sequences). Was there some subject that, as I wrote, I kept thinking about including? (Maybe you should have.)

- What areas seem weak?
  Have I shortchanged on logic somewhere? Is this passage murky? Does this chart make its point?

- What should I cut?
  What parts seem too long, or repetitious, or irrelevant, or somehow damaging to the company, or the argument?

- How smooth are the transitions?
  Does one section suggest the next? Do I provide the information needed *when* it's needed—and not three sections later?

Once you've added, subtracted, patched, and smoothed, you have cleared up your organization, and in the process gotten rid of a lot of the tangled paragraphs.

Your next reading should be word by word. Only now should you bother crossing out one word and penciling in a better one. Only now should you worry about following the format conventions demanded by your company.

Essentially, at this stage you're following up on the ideas we've been talking about throughout "A Plain Style." For instance, now is the time to start turning passive constructions into active ones, changing vague phrases into specific references, shortening, sharpening.

Specifically, you check:

SPELLING. Check especially names, addresses, and unusual terms.

GRAMMAR. Are sentences complete? Do your verbs agree with their subjects in number?

USAGE. Do you use standard English? Have you looked up phrases you're not sure of?

FORMAT. Are your margins wide enough? Does each page look open and inviting?

MATH. Have you made sure your results are arithmetically correct?

CONSISTENCY. Are all the headings in one section presented in parallel form? Does the table of contents match the headings?

All these changes are important, but only make them when they support your new organization and make it clearer. Throughout, keep one question in mind: will this change help the reader understand my main point?

Once you've cleaned up the prose in the document, clean up the way it looks. Retype or print it out again. Then put *that* version away for a few days, so you can get more distance. Then go back through it one more time, revising. The order, then the style.

Two run-throughs should be enough. If you find you're doing more than that, something's not right. Perhaps your ideas have matured, or perhaps the situation itself has shifted. Maybe you're the victim of bosses or colleagues who are changing their minds. Or you just like tinkering.

Don't revise in order to make the document "perfect"— that takes too long. Make it good enough. Too much revision can be worse than none.

□ BEFRIEND YOUR WORD PROCESSOR (IF YOU HAVE ONE) □

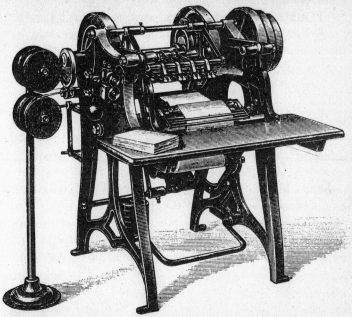

||||||||||||||||||||||||||||||||||||||||||||||||||||||||||||||||||||||||||||||

When I use a pen, I find I have so much time between each word that I can edit as I go. My writing is condensed. When I type, I can put the letters down so fast I tend to write too much. Afterward, I leave them there—it seems like too much work to retype. Word processing offers me both—speedy drafts and easy editing.

To write this book I'm using a word processing program on my Apple ///. But I still like pens. What's as cozy as you in an armchair with a pen and pad, scribbling away? No clacking keys, no blinking screen—just pages flipping off your lap.

But even if someone else can read your draft and type it, revising can get tedious. We all know the arrows, interlinings, inserts, cross-hatchings, and tracery. The tangle slows the typist down, and doesn't help you think straight, either.

And learning to use a word processor, or getting material through a word processing center, can drive anyone crazy for a while. But management's going to bring in word processing anyway—most research shows it saves money.

If you fight word processing, you're going to lose. Your reports will come out late, garbled, messy. So even if you still take notes with your pen, learn to live with word processing.

Sure, in the beginning, dealing with computers can make anyone feel like going back to a quill pen. If you key in the text yourself, you've probably run into infuriating inconsistencies in the commands, puzzling balks, sudden wipe-outs, file foul-ups. Suddenly the machine refuses to do what it's done before. Your title comes out of the printer draped across three pages, and the rest of the text gets scrambled so it looks like alphabet soup. And just when you need that letter, the printer breaks.

How could you befriend a machine like that? First, recognize that your initial experience with a word processor will be irritating, no matter which system you're getting acquainted with. Each system has its own rather peculiar way it wants you to enter text, give orders, or move files around. And what works at some stage won't work at another. (That's because the people who wrote the program probably had very little idea of what you go through when you have to write English.)

If you are going to use a word processor, you can make your life easier by pestering the dealer or manufacturer. First of all, demand a manual. Don't settle for promises that it will come several weeks after the system's installed. If you get the manual and it's missing any of the following, insist these elements be provided: index; glossary; tutorial (step-by-step basics); detailed reference on each function; and quick reference card.

Next, demand real training—not just a pamphlet and a pat on the back, or even a cassette tape, with more paper. Insist on real people you can talk to. Make sure you have someone you can call when you're in the middle of a letter and can't figure out how to get the machine to center a heading. Find buddies at work; track down someone human at the dealer or manufacturer. For even more help, you can look in computer stores, bookstores, and libraries for any introductory texts.

As you get started on word processing, learn to do your "housekeeping" regularly. Until you put your text into a more permanent memory, your work is stored only in the memory of your computer or terminal, which goes blank the moment the electrical power goes off. Every ten minutes or so, save your text on disk or tape; then you can reconstruct it later. That way, if the lights go out, you won't lose all the work you've done that day.

There are other maintenance chores that will help keep your system from getting clogged up or misused. Go through your files every few weeks and purge the material you'll never use again: birthday congratulations; requests for a subscription; a personal letter. If your system requires that you format a disk before you use it, format ten or twenty so that you're never stuck with a ten-page letter on the computer, and no place to put it. If you're going to need something a year from now, put it on a disk or tape, and store that. Don't keep it on your main computer or on disks you use a lot—that just wastes space. Wipe out notes and any documents that could be embarrassing. If you leave them on the system, the wrong person may find a way to get into your files, and read them—at the wrong time. Also, set the security codes so that nobody else can rewrite your report without your permission.

Above all, don't get into the hunkered-down pose. Some people get so shell-shocked by their initial experiences with a word processor that they never go beyond the basic functions. These people accept absurd limitations rather than explore the word processor's advanced functions. One man I know spent eight months turning out triple-spaced memos because he knew how——and he didn't dare try out the command that let him do single-spacing.

So set aside time to explore the fancy extras that come with the system. Think of it this way: you've paid a lot of money for conveniences that you're not using.

On the other hand, don't *overuse* the functions that word processing makes possible, such as the "copy" command. Yes, you can use it to take a paragraph you put in Section One, and copy it over in Sections Three, Five, and Eighteen. But the reader will notice, and you'll begin to sound like a machine.

Certainly, word processing makes revisions easy. But don't act like the engineers who, realizing that, wrote sloppier first drafts than ever on the theory that it wouldn't be hard to revise them later. Quality went down, and all the time that management anticipated would be saved by going to word processing was lost, since the engineers now had to go through five or six drafts to get a final report.

If you deal with word processing operators, try to make the work they do for you as straightforward and uncomplicated as possible. Studies show that people who have to work at a cathode ray tube all day have more anxiety, high blood pressure, and stress-related disease than any other occupation, including air traffic controllers. And then your manuscript comes in, marked "Urgent——Need ASAP."

You can help out the operator——and increase the chances that you'll get back clean copy——if you take the time to:

- Print, if you must write by hand. Speak up if you're dictating. Don't make the operator spend minutes guessing whether you meant *library* or *liberty*.
- Learn the formats that are possible with your system and stick to them. Avoid weird margins, odd headings, strange type fonts.
- Write a cover note explaining which format you want to use. If there's a standard one for memos, letters,

reports, say you want it. Don't depend on the operator to figure out that it is a memo. Also, specify any variations.

- Use whatever proofreading marks the operators know.

- Make a real effort to meet the person who does your word processing. Talk with him or her as you hand in each new job. Go over what you want. Compare this job with other ones that person's done for you. Make friends—your document depends on it.

- Realize that some jobs are tricky. For instance, you can't easily send text from one word processing system to another. (Often the text comes through, but all the commands you used to arrange it on the page get fouled up.)

- Set realistic deadlines. You may not have as high a priority as the boss, so your letter can't get done today. Leave comfortable time margins for return of your document.

Basically, the more you know about the word processing system you are using and the conditions under which the operators must work, the easier you'll find it to steer your document past disasters. And when you get all those neat letters, accurate reports, fast memos, you may even start to smile when you look at your word processor.

▪ *Common Tasks* ▪

□ *MEMOS* □

ost memos are too ornate—even when they're not written with a quill pen. Too many words, too little point. Executives who have to read dozens of memos every day react like this:

"It's not clear what I'm supposed to do about this."
"What's the point?"

"I know there's a problem, but what does this guy think should be done about it?"

"I didn't just want facts—I wanted her opinion."

Before you write, think out your aim. If you're not clear about that, your reader won't be. What do you want your memo to do?

- To get action: persuade the boss to okay your new plan; set a deadline and schedule for a group; confirm what you will do, and what you expect others to do.
- To avoid blame: "report" the facts, while justifying yourself, or "make your case" in the files.
- To answer a question: make an argument for your ideas, under the guise of a neutral report; or say what policy you recommend.

So Make a Point

Show what you expect your reader to do next—approve your idea, blame someone else, okay your budget. Even when someone has asked you to "just outline the situation," they are likely to ask for your suggestions. Save time and put them in writing now.

Of course, saying what you think commits you to a position. You have to take a stand and not weasel out of it halfway through or mound up so much mush around your idea that no one will ever spot it again. (Cowardice breeds bad writing as its camouflage.) Be brave enough to make a real point.

Rewrite

Many people think a memo's just a note, so they can ramble on and on and touch on this and that and exit leaving a pile of words behind. In fact, dictation encourages meandering memos like this:

MEMORANDUM

DATE: December 10

TO: Dan Knipper   FROM: Mel Burrows

SUBJECT: Marketing Meeting

Way back last October when we first got around to planning this meeting, I thought I would be back from the NCA conference—it's going to be in Hawaii this year, thank God—I'm looking forward to getting a good tan, too. Well, anyway, I figured I could easily be back in town by the 21st, but now I've got to stop off in Los Angeles on the way back, to talk to some of our subcontractors on the Galaxy Project. So I'm not sure now whether I will be back by the 21st, or even the 22nd. I'm just not sure how bad the situation is there. So what about the 23rd? Nobody really wants to meet on Christmas eve, right? I've tried reaching you on the phone, but your secretary couldn't speak to your schedule, so I figured I'd better send you this. Let me know what's best for you. Of course, when I get in, I'll be brushing sand off me. Know any good restaurants in Honolulu?

Try reducing that to two sentences—or one. You can cross out 90 percent of what's there. That done, the point emerges. And with a few changes, you've got a memo someone can answer without spending five minutes following the twists and turns of Mel's free-associating mind.

Remember, it takes longer to say something briefly—you have to cut out so much. So figure on revising two or three times, if you want the reader to grasp your idea quickly, and act on it.

Give the Reader Air

White space helps. Open up the page so the reader's eye can zoom in on key parts, without getting stalled by a big block of type.

When possible, use headings to break up the text. With lists, spread out the items with bullets or numbers, and let some blank lines sneak in between them.

Here's one memo that started as a clump. See how much easier it is to skim after the text has been given some breathing room.

BEFORE:

MEMORANDUM

DATE: December 12

TO: Jim Brandon　　　　　　FROM: Mel Burrows

SUBJECT: Contract with CDN-Nippon

We should give our drive-shaft contract to CDN. The main benefits: they have the longest experience with this particular engineering, they have manufactured more of this model than anyone else, they are offering us a price 12% below any of their competitors; plus, we've worked with them before, and found their failure rate to stay consistently below 3%. The drawbacks: a month delay in startup, due to their previous commitments, and a guarantee of first option on the next contract. Our lawyers say these conditions are OK. So let's sign.

AFTER:

MEMORANDUM

DATE: December 12

TO: Jim Brandon　　　　　　FROM: Mel Burrows

SUBJECT: Contract with CDN-Nippon

We should give our drive-shaft contract to CDN.

THE BENEFITS:

—They have the longest experience with this particular engineering.

—They have manufactured more of this model than anyone else.

—Their price is 12% below the lowest competitor.

—We've worked with them before.

—Their failure rate is consistently below 3%.

THE DRAWBACKS:

—A one-month delay, due to their previous commitments.

—They want a guarantee of first option on our next contract.

CONCLUSION:

Our lawyers give the OK. Let's sign.

Use Familiar Organization

To speed your reader's access to your main point, follow a traditional way of organizing your material: problem and solution; main idea and proofs; and effect and causes. The reader will recognize each of these arrangements quickly, and will know where to look for your recommended course of action.

Steer clear of a simple-minded plod through events in chronological or geographical order—easy for you, but hard on the reader. Such lists exhaust themselves without building to a conclusion. They leave the reader wondering what you make of all this information—and why you're asking him or her to wade through it.

Put Your Key Idea First

Basically, move from the most important to the least important. A memo is not an opera, a cocktail conversation, or a nineteenth-century novel.

So put your idea in the first sentence. And if your company's memo pads offer you a subject line, put your idea there. If your memo stretches more than a page, you need a summary at the top. Not just a statement of the topic ("In this memo I will discuss . . ."), but a stand ("We should eliminate the Dallas plant because . . ."). And even a one-paragraph memo becomes clearer—works faster—when you start with the point.

Don't begin with the background, sidling up to your subject ("The purpose of this memo . . ."), or with elaborate definitions, warnings about the scope of the memo to come, personal remarks (unless you've got nothing else to say). If you must include any of this, put it below your opening. Subordinate the insignificant to the meaningful.

Make a Definite Recommendation

Go beyond analysis to say what you think the reader—and you—should do next. This makes the memo a trigger for action, not just another excuse for delay.

Sometimes you know what should be done, but you don't want to do it. Or you know that to decide, you need to collect some figures or interview an expert. If you're putting off that work, then you'll resist making any clear recommendation in your memo. Here's what you'll sound like:

MEMORANDUM

DATE: December 8

TO: Vice President Merker   FROM: Mel Burrows

SUBJECT: Disk Drive Failures

We have had problems with defective disk drives. This has been going on for a year. At first, we thought we could just change our manufacturing procedures, but that led to even more failures. We're now getting less than 20% of the product past Quality Assurance. Now we could go back to engineering, and ask for a new de-

sign, but that might take six months or a year. Or we
could go out and buy a different drive right off the shelf.
Or we could just manufacture an awful lot of them, so
we could use the 20% that work. I'm not sure whether
Manufacturing can handle that kind of volume. What do
you think? We've got to do something soon, to meet our
shipments.

"We've got to do something now." Sure, but it won't be
done too fast. At least, not by Mel.

Before you write, then, take the time to do what any
reader's probably going to tell you to do. Talk to the manufacturing people. Research the subject enough so you can make a
considered recommendation. And ask yourself: am I prepared
to act on my own recommendation? If not, revise it.

Make It Even Shorter

When you've got a first draft, go through it looking for parts
to cut. Can you shrink a paragraph to a line or two? Do so, and
you've chopped away some of the underbrush, so a reader can
spot your ideas right off. Avoid this sort of thing:

MEMORANDUM

DATE: December 31

TO: Hank Holquist   FROM: Mel Burrows

SUBJECT: Length of Memoranda

It has come to my attention, from various sources,
that some people have the feeling that our company
memos are getting a little long-winded. Now I don't op-
pose a little detail, and I always want to hear what you
have to say, but I'd like you to issue a general memorandum warning people to keep the length of all but the
most important or well-researched memos short, so we
don't have to spend all day reading them. If you know
what I mean.

Get Out Fast

Stop before your memo becomes a full-dress research paper. At the bottom of the page there should be no more than the typist's initials, and an alphabetized distribution list, if it's too long to be put on the "to" line. No "sincerely yours," and no flourishes.

If you're stapling on attachments, fine, but make sure you've described them in the memo, so the reader's prepared. And ask yourself: is this really a part of my presentation? Or is it just decoration? If it is just extra weight, leave it out.

A Memo on Memos

MEMORANDUM

DATE: February 15

TO: You

FROM: Jonathan Price

SUBJECT: How to Write Memos

Put your main point at the start!

- Rewrite.
- Give the reader air.
- Use familiar organization.
- Put your key idea first.
- Make a definite recommendation.
- Make it even shorter.
- Get out fast.

□ *LETTERS* □

|||||||||||||||||||||||||||||||||||||||||||||||||||||||||||||||||||||||||||||||||||||||||||

Is this how you subconsciously see the person who'll be getting your letter? Some old guy who's got so many hours free that he doesn't know what to do with them all? Someone who's going to read your letter from beginning to end three times, just rocking on the porch?

If so, you'll probably let yourself write a long, rambling letter, in which you leave it up to him to guess what you really want. And since he's in a listening mood, you might also indulge yourself in some sharp, negative, vicious, or pompous comments—insider jokes, putdowns, and worries. You'll get a lot off your chest, and you imagine he'll read it all like a father, understanding just what you need, and responding by return mail.

This is fantasy. You're lucky if any recipient reads your whole letter. It's better to imagine someone opening your envelope in the elevator; reading the letter in the hall; putting coffee on it, right on your key paragraph; losing it for a few days; handing it to a colleague, but forgetting to make a copy; and then calling you a week later with only a vague memory of your letter.

That's the worst case. I recommend preparing your letter so it can make an impact, even if it suffers this fate.

Once you learn a different way of thinking about letters, you'll find they go faster, and get better response. The first step: put off the actual writing.

Understand Why You're Writing

This seems obvious, but it isn't. There are numerous half-thought-out reasons for letters. Among them: because they asked me for a report on the situation. (Sure they did. But you have a point to make, a deal to clinch. Keep that in mind.) Or, because I said I would write. (You can't remember why. Well, why do you care about these people? What do you want them to do for you?) Or, because they're angry. (Turn the anger into an additional sale. Don't just think of this letter as a defense attorney's brief.)

Figure out what positive benefit you can get out of a letter. You can keep an old customer, or make a new one. Get someone to ship you something, right away. Give credit, in order to secure a large order. Persuade someone to stop pestering you.

If you think in terms of an actual result, you'll be able to write a clear letter aiming for it. Think aggressively, then, before you write. What's in it for you?

Of course, sometimes you'll have no immediate goal in mind. But you can make people feel good if you send them a short note, such as when you hear any news about them personally, such as birthdays, graduations, moves, promotions; or when you have a chance to thank them for a small favor, or a piece of information they passed along; or when you notice something nice about their product.

These letters help maintain good will, but they are not trivial. They prepare the way for the more important letters.

Incidentally, you could probably write more letters. I know that sounds like a horrible idea. How could you find the time? But you'll definitely stand out from most of your colleagues if you do keep in touch with a lot of letters.

Don't write a lot, then, but write often. Keep people up to date. Create a tickler file, or make notes on your calendar, reminding you that it's time to get in touch with people. Even if you've talked to them by phone, confirm what you said in a note. That gives you a written record (the lawyers will appreciate that, if you have trouble later) and a convenient way to show how you interpreted the slightly ambiguous grunts and hums on the line.

State Your Business in Your First Paragraph

A lot of letters leave you wondering what they're about. One way to make that clear at the start is a heading. For instance, right after the salutation, you could put something like this:

Dear Ed:

Recommending Approval of the Downtown Site

A heading like this will help Ed focus his mind. He's probably been thinking about something other than you and your downtown site. And the heading will help you later, when you are leafing through thirty or forty different letters to Ed, trying to find the one about the downtown site.

Notice that your heading can do more than state a topic. You can use the heading to recommend an action or answer a question.

Your first paragraph should be bold: say what you want there. I know this may seem impolite, but actually it helps the reader know where you stand, without having to wonder about it for five paragraphs. Also, you get your main point across before they stop reading, and that alone may encourage them to read more.

Don't lead up to your idea. Don't strike a neutral pose, as if you were a scientist reporting the result. Don't leave your main point for the last paragraph.

NOT A SLOW BEGINNING,

At your request, I have made a preliminary investigation of the reasons our sales force has lost out to the competition in at least a dozen cases, despite the fact that our proposal came in lower overall. I talked with each sales representative, and with eight of the potential customers. From my research, I have begun to come up with some tentative conclusions about possible solutions to this puzzling problem.

A MAIN POINT, RIGHT OFF

Let's Quote High, Then Discount

We should resume our industry's practice of quoting a high price, then discounting that. This lets purchasers feel they are getting a good deal, and that they have proven their business skills. We've lost at least six sales worth more than $8.3 million because we quoted high and would not discount.

If you're afraid your correspondents may have forgotten that they asked you for some information, refer to their letter by date and give a brief summary of what they said. That can help them get back on track. But don't devote more than a sentence or two to this, and keep it from interfering with your main message.

Show Why What You're Saying Is Important to Your Readers

Diagnose your main point. Why should the readers care?

- You're going to solve a problem for them.
- You've found a way for them to save money.
- If they give you the information you want, you can reciprocate with some from your files.
- You're going to help them make a profit.
- They'll feel great when they respond to your request.

Somehow, you need to devote some of your early paragraphs to these reasons for reading on. The longer your letter, the more you need these advertisements at the beginning.

In Confirming an Agreement, Quote Exactly What Was Said

During important phone calls or meetings, get in the habit of writing down all key points, quoting yourself and the other people. This takes a little extra concentration, but it will help you later, when you come to write the letter that will get it down on paper.

Learn to pay particular attention to the way other people phrase touchy or dangerous parts of an agreement. You know those areas could cause conflict later. So record their very words—that way, even the most argumentative person will have to accept your summary of the conversation.

Also, in the letter, spell out your understanding of even the most ambiguous parts of the agreement. If you don't do it now, the lawyers may have to later.

And don't forget to confirm those "obvious" details such as the date, place, and hour of the next meeting, the total budget you are talking about, the response you expect, and the deadline you have set.

Take Responsibility for What You Are Saying

Nothing's more infuriating than a letter turning down a request because of some "policy" or "company standard." So don't shift the blame. As far as your reader's concerned, it's your decision. So say "I." Then, if you really feel it's important, explain that you're following a policy. That way, they don't feel you're an oily bureaucrat or, worse, a manager who's bound and gagged by outworn rules.

If you're responding to a complaint, and you feel it was justified, say so. Admit that you, or your company, fouled up. That alone will make the customer happier, since we all *expect* the brush-off.

Show that you—a real person—understand their point of view. Say something like:

Dear Mrs. Peterson,

I'd be upset, too, at the way we messed up your order of Waterford crystal. I'm sorry we sent the wrong glasses, and broke them in the process. Just throw those pieces away. I've asked our shipping department to get the right set out to you today.

You should be receiving those by the week of May 23rd, via United Parcel. If you have any questions, please call me collect.

Of course, taking responsibility for what you say may mean you have to do some work before you write—like calling the shipping department, and making sure they do get that new set out. When you find you're putting off a letter, ask yourself if it's because you don't like writing, or working.

Go the Extra Mile—So the Reader Doesn't Have To

You can always just answer somebody's question, and let them take it from there. But how much more helpful you can be if you think about the situation from their point of view, and suggest what they could do next. For instance, when you've finished the letter as far as you're concerned, pause for a moment to think about questions like these:

- What information will my reader want to know now? Do I have it, or can I get it?
- Who else will my reader want informed? Could I send them copies of this letter?
- What will my reader's next step probably be? How can I make that easier?
- If I'm saying no, who might say yes? If I don't know the answer, who might?

When you take the time to provide the extra information, you keep your letter from settling like uncooked dough in the reader's stomach. Your thoughtfulness will make most readers look forward to your next letter. And it may even make your job a little easier next week, when the reader would normally call back for that extra piece of information. If there's a deal brewing, you may have speeded it up by a week or more.

Another way to pack a little more in each letter: think of each letter, even an answer to a complaint, as a chance to do a little selling. For instance, responding to a customer's gripes about slow delivery, you might admit that your delivery's been bad, but point out that this is because you've gotten so many orders for your new widget—more than you expected. So your customer might want to assure a steady supply by ordering replacements now.

Be Definite about What You Want

Lots of letters leave the question of what you want murky. Perhaps their writers feel embarrassed to ask, or guilty for wanting so much. By hiding their demand under purple prose, they confuse the reader, and don't often get what they want.

Thin out the nervous qualifiers like "I hope that," "It may possibly be the case that," and "I would certainly imagine that."

Say what you expect the reader to do. Say it in the beginning, spell out the details in the middle, and if your letter goes more than a page, say it briefly at the end.

Include all the details the reader will need to carry out your request. For instance:

- account numbers, Social Security numbers, invoice numbers, file numbers;
- dates of important letters, forms, meetings;
- full names of everyone who might be involved, along with addresses and phone numbers—including numbers where they can be reached at night or on weekends;
- deadline for delivery—along with the place and person who'll be receiving.

The more data you put in, the fewer excuses the reader will have to put off acting on your request. And that means a lot fewer phone calls later.

Make Your Closing Count

Avoid slow fades. Too many letters take back what the writer said, in an earnest effort to keep the peace. Watch out for reversing yourself with last paragraphs like these:

- Of course, that's just what our marketing people think. I'm sure there are plenty of other points of view. I hope we can reason together on this. [Mushy: what do you think?]

- I guess this means we'll all have to look into the subject a little more. No one's blaming you, Bill. They
  just have been wondering what you've been up to, all
  these weeks in Hawaii. Now I've told them you're
  going to sell the Army on our Rest and Recreation
  package, but I wonder if you could explain this other
  matter to them. On the other hand, maybe it will all
  blow over. [Again, where do you stand?]

If you're really uncertain, resolve your doubts before you
write. Or define the question you're unsure about, and ask the
reader to help you by answering it.

Resist the conventional charm at the end. If you really know
the person, sure, put in some personal notes. But don't manufacture sentiment, even in your "Sincerely yours." For instance, if you've just complained for six paragraphs, don't
switch to saccharin all of a sudden, wishing them all the best
for the holiday season.

If you'd blush saying something in person, don't write it.
When you don't know how to end the letter, here are some
quick closes:

- Say when you expect to hear from them next.
- Sketch out what you think the long-range benefits of
  this project will be.
- Sum up what you think about the subject.
- Tell a story that illustrates your main point.

Revise for Looks

This procedure is definitely worth the effort, even if you
have to retype the copy a couple of times. Here are a few
guidelines:

- Center the letter so the bulk of your text falls at that
  point halfway between top to bottom.
- Leave plenty of room for your signature. If it comes

too close to the bottom, start lower on the first page, and put at least one paragraph on the last page.

- Use wide margins. An inch and a half on all sides.
- Use a new ribbon—film, if possible—on your typewriter. Avoid sending dot-matrix computer printout outside of your company; use letter-quality printers instead.
- Make sure you're sending out the best stationery if you're writing to people outside the company.

For short notes of congratulations or thanks, go ahead and use a pen. That looks more personal. Of course, if your handwriting's as bad as mine, you'd better go back to typing.

Add a (Pleasant) Surprise

Surprise the reader with a little bonus—something that's relevant to your subject, but not expected. A gift. Possibilities include an extra brochure, a photo, an offprint of a recent review of your products, or your company's regular calendar, ruler, pen, or gimcrack. It's not so much what you send, as the fact that you bother to put in what Winnie the Pooh used to call "a little something."

Be Different

In general, people put off writing letters as long as they can and send as few as possible, and each one is confused but unhelpful. You can make your own letters stand out from the rest of the mail by adopting what I call the "extra" attitude. A clear, direct letter requires that you put in a lot more work before writing than a fuzzy, rambling, incoherent letter would take. But clarity and directness will speed up decisions, help out the reader, and win you a lot of that old intangible: good will.

Think of the letters you receive, and then you'll see why I think you'll stand out if you do what we've talked about:

- Understand why you're writing.
- State your business in your first paragraph.
- Show why what you're saying is important to your readers.
- In confirming an agreement, quote exactly what was said.
- Take responsibility for what you are saying.
- Go the extra mile—so the reader doesn't have to.
- Be definite about what you want.
- Make your closing count.
- Revise for looks.
- Add a (pleasant) surprise.
- Be different.

||||||||||||||||||||||||||||||||||||||||||||||||||||||||||||||||||||||||||||||||||||||||||

Most reports—like most letters—take too long to get to the point. You can tell that the writers spent a lot of time coiling ropes, scraping barnacles, collecting specimens, and looking at the stars. But for all that preparation, you wonder what they were after. You can see the sweat: but where's the whale?

Here's how some people react to all that work:

- "I couldn't figure out what they were driving at."
- "I couldn't find the stuff I was after."
- "I didn't read it, I weighed it."
- "What can I do about it? I never found any recommendations I could act on."
- "Why did they bring in all those statistics?"
- "Oh yes, I read it. Now what was that about?"

Reports and proposals keep getting balled up like that partly because we go on making some false assumptions about our audiences. We imagine they care as much as we do about the subject. We figure they know a lot about it, too; in fact, they're such experts that they'll catch us making the slightest exaggeration, and they'll criticize us if we don't include every minor exception. Furthermore, they understand all the unstated implications, the political overtones, so there's no need to spell any of those things out. Because our audience is so fascinated, they're willing to wait to the end for our point.

In most cases, these assumptions are wrong. You face a diverse group of readers, from decision-makers who don't want to know details down to nit-pickers who couldn't care less about your overall idea. So write for the different groups within your audience. The beginning is for people who only have time to skim. The middle is for people who want to know more—but not everything. The back matter (appendices, tables, index) helps out the real experts. And remember there are very few of these.

For the nonexperts—two-thirds of your audience, usually—make your main point clear right off. If you think you don't *have* a main point, better look at your research again.

Realize that you have to show people why they should care about your report. What's in it for them? Plan to show why most people—not just experts—will find the key points useful. Ask yourself questions.

Are you recommending a plan that will save or make a lot of money? Increase productivity? Improve the morale of hundreds of employees?

Are you telling them about the success or failure of recent efforts, with an explanation that points to improvements you could make?

Have you thought through your main point enough that you can express it in a way that appeals to the self-interest of most of your audience?

Make an Argument

You can't "just report the facts." Your opinion will shape them, whether you acknowledge that or not. And in fact, most reports and proposals become useful only when you lead off with a clearly stated main idea—an argument.

So figure out where you stand. If you're not sure, do one of these things:

- Take a position.
- Recommend an action.
- Disagree with someone, and show how you would redo their analysis.
- Translate a budget into meaningful terms.
- Sum up the gist of your plan.
- Decide what's the most important item in your analysis.
- State your conclusions in the way you would to a friend—someone who's sympathetic, but doesn't want to hear all the details.

Another way to figure out your main point is to decide what results you want from the report. Write that down on a piece of paper, and post that over your desk. Examples: "Win approval of my budget and plan"; "Get promoted to senior manager"; and "Get the boss and his staff to cancel the MH Project."

When you know what results you want, you can organize the rest of your report to persuade your audience to vote that way.

Ask a Lot of Questions

Work backward from the result you want to the main point you'll make, and from there to the facts you need to discover to support your case. Yes, that sounds backward. But in fact, you'll save a lot of research time if you start with your idea, then look for the facts that will help you prove it.

Of course you should keep your eye open to facts that tend to disprove your main idea. If they are trivial, you can dismiss them in footnotes. If potentially damaging, you can bring them up in the body of your text, then show why they don't really disprove your point. That way you sound reasonable, but consistent. If these facts, however, are important, perhaps you'd better rethink your main point, or offer major qualifications ("Of course, this all depends on sales surpassing our quota, and that may not happen.").

But knowing what you're after will let you dismiss a lot of the vaguely relevant material you might feel compelled to read if you were really writing a report that dealt with *everything* about this topic. You're luckier; you just need data to support or refine your idea. That's a lot less than everything.

Another way to find out what to look up is to anticipate the questions your audience might ask themselves when listening to each part of your argument. For instance:

- What's the problem? What's your solution?
- How much will all this cost? How do those costs break down, anyway?
- What are the stages? Do you have a schedule, with milestones and budget?
- What kind of effects can we anticipate, based on similar projects in the past?

- Who will do what—and why them?
- How many alternatives have been considered? And why did you reject them?
- What risks are involved? What opportunities?
- How important is this to your group, division, whole company?
- What impact could this have on current plans? How does your plan fit in with the broader company goals?
- What are the full details on capabilities, limits, quantities?
- What kind of errors, slowdowns, failures, botches, conflicts can we anticipate?

Organize in a Recognizable Order

When organizing your material, try to fit it into a pattern most people can recognize. For instance, problem, then solution; most important idea, then less important ones; or what happened first, then after, then last.

You can also begin with the situation seen up close as it affects your immediate office, then as it affects the division, then as it affects the whole company. Or you can point out a danger looming over all of us in the company, then explain what you think should be done to escape it.

Early in your work, make some notes and try to organize your whole report in one of these familiar ways. Later, you'll see ways you can organize individual sections similarly.

Since readers can see how you are organizing your report, they don't have to waste time and energy figuring that out. They won't get lost. They can see why each part appears, and how the pieces fit together into a persuasive argument. The more visible your structure, the clearer your point will be.

At the Very Beginning, Spotlight Your Main Point

No matter what pattern you fit your material into, lead off with your main idea. In fact, you can make your title do extra work. Take a sentence summing up your main idea, then turn that into a title.

NOT A BLAND TITLE,	*AN IDEA*
Report from the Budget Committee	Why We Should Change our Auditors
Results of the 1983 Study of Sales of All Models, with Emphasis on the Compact	Saving Our Compact Model

Make your table of contents talk, too. A lot of these just list sections, as if everyone would want to look up Section Three. So turn your section titles into phrases that hint at the contents—and your point of view. Like this:

NOT A TRADITIONAL SECTION HEADING,	*AN INFORMATIVE ONE*
Section 1	I. The Problem: Falling Prices, Rising Costs
Part II, Section 2.3	Why the Swedish Approach Won't Work Today
Section 2-C	Our Best Course of Action: 33 Ways to Cut Costs

A lot of reports start with the table of contents, then ramble through half a dozen pages of prefaces. Cut these out. They're anachronisms, left over from the days when people had a few hours to read each report that came across their desks. They postpone your message, waste readers' time, build a wall of verbiage between them and you.

Of course, if your company—or your client—insists on some of these throat-clearing sections, go ahead and put them in, but find some way to tie each in to your main point. Here's how:

SUMMARY, OR ABSTRACT. Your chance to trumpet your main idea in the first sentence, followed by key supporting evidence, in one paragraph. If your abstracts also highlight key words, add the ones that most people in your company would use to sum up the topic, and your approach to it. (A key word helps future researchers look up all the abstracts that carry that label.)

HISTORY. Keep it brief, and show how it all leads up to the problem you're about to solve. Edit out the irrelevant events. Create a direct line from one key moment up to your present report. Show how all history cries out for your report.

STATEMENT OF PURPOSE. Usually folderol designed to make your report sound important. Instead, say what you're investigating—and the way you say that can tip a smart reader off to your conclusions.

NEED. Why the report is needed. As with the history section, this one just begs for you to show why this report is needed. If you're solving a problem, outline the consequences of not solving it. Quote authorities, state dollar volumes.

METHOD OF RESEARCH. Keep it short, but make it sound exhaustive. (Details belong in the body of your report, or in an appendix.) You're showing how much evidence supports your main point. You may also want to cast doubt on the research methods of people known to disagree with you.

SCOPE. Rule out whatever an innocent reader might mistake your report for. If you have restricted yourself to a study of your division's problems, explain that you have not investigated any other division.

DEFINITION OF TERMS. Only put in the definitions for terms you think the boss might get confused about. And no more than ten. Send people to your glossary for any others. Be sure to define any unusual term you're including in your main point.

Sort Details Out by Audience Level

Most of your research findings will end up in the middle of your report. As you approach each section, recognize that a lot of your readers—particularly the decision-makers—will be skimming through. Help these people out by including brief summaries at the beginning of each new piece of evidence. That way they can read the summaries, and skip the details.

When you're describing stages of a process, number the steps, include pictures where possible, and leave plenty of room between steps, so readers can digest the material of one step before moving on to the next. If you have a lot of steps, put lines between them. That way, people who aren't familiar with the process can follow along. Even experts can stand a clear explanation.

At the end of any section of evidence, be sure to sum up how this all relates to the main theme of the chapter, and the report. Don't count on most readers seeing the connection. You do, because you've been immersed in the subject. But a newcomer can't always see the relevance. And don't worry about being repetitious; few people are reading your whole report, anyway.

Design your report for the convenience of the casual reader, and the thorough one will appreciate it, too.

Sell Your Proposal

If you're proposing a solution to a client's problem, or a new plan for your own company, you'll spend most of your time figuring out details of your technical or administrative solutions—specifications, test dates, evaluation procedures, reporting paths, feedback techniques, schedules, budgets. All that's intriguing, but the reader is going to want to know why your ideas are better than everyone else's.

Your report must act as a sales letter, showing the unique benefits of your idea. Sum them up in the first few pages, then devote whole sections to them. These benefits are what will convince the nonexpert that your plan has value. The details blur before their eyes—that's why they hire experts, to check.

Decision-makers take a longer view: they want to know why you've got a better idea than your competition. They're looking for evidence like this: cost justification; return on investment, amortized over various periods; major benefits of your plan; half a dozen reasons to discard other plans; answers to major worries—mean time between failure, service contracts, guarantees, safety records; reliability of your research, of your group, of the vendors you're planning to solicit.

Put details like this in your first chapter, then devote other sections to the details *behind* them. The schedules and budgets are simply extra information, supporting these key points.

Make It Easy to Move Around

If your report or proposal threatens to go longer than ten pages, you'll want to make sure that someone who doesn't know the field intimately can find a particular fact quickly. That means you may have to annotate your table of contents, add a real glossary of terms, and make up an index.

Usually, your table of contents just mentions chapter headings and page numbers. But in a longer report, you should distinguish between several layers of heading, like this:

A MAJOR ONE

An Important One

A) A Minor Heading

Then include your important headings in the main table of contents. And set up a separate table of contents for each chapter, reaching down to the lowest level of heading. That way the main contents let a reader skim by general topic; the chapter contents help him or her find specific information.

Your naive readers will wonder what some of your terms mean. Sure, you define them when you first mention them. But then they get to page fifty, wonder what this gizmo is, and can't find where you first brought it up. That's where your glossary can help. Define every term that your most inexperienced— but important—reader will want to know. Put the alphabetical list of definitions in the back, but alert readers to its existence on the first page.

And, definitely include an index. You won't know page numbers until you get a final draft. But right from the start, you can be making up a list of terms to include. Every time you show someone a draft, pass them the index, and ask them to see if you've included everything they might look up. You'll be testing your index the only way that counts: on real readers.

Yes, Come to a Real Conclusion

At the end, readers expect you'll tell them what you've concluded. Too many writers simply call for further study or voice alarm. Restate your main recommendations.

Highlight the most important idea you want to get across. If you have a number of other recommendations, subordinate those; group them by type; number them within the groups. If you do have a lot of recommendations, order the groups logically——by time, by department, by area.

Do anything you can to avoid a bland, unassertive ending. Insist on your main point. That's the result of all this thinking you've just been paid to do. You may feel a little loud, a bit repetitious, because you've heard it before——but this may be the first time your boss or client understands what you're driving at.

So here are my recommendations:

- Make an argument.
- Ask a lot of questions.
- Organize in a recognizable order.
- At the very beginning, spotlight your main point.
- Sort details out by audience level.
- Sell your proposal.
- Make it easy to move around.
- Yes, come to a real conclusion!

☐ *SPEECHES* ☐

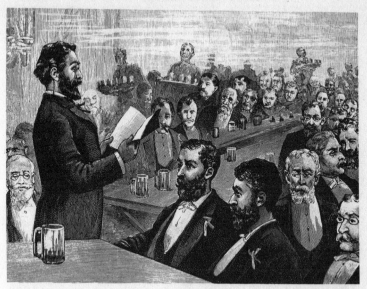

Is anyone listening? You may never have to read a lecture to a crowded bar, but you probably have to make impromptu explanations in meetings, brief harangues for right-thinking, little sermons, sales pitches, even a few formal presentations. For the moment, think of these all as speeches. And contemplate the fact that most speeches—of any kind—end up boring the audience.

When asked about a recent presentation, audience members who had applauded politely at the end said—off the record, and anonymously—

> "It was too long."
>
> "I couldn't see any point in it. It was just rambling."
>
> "Well, I could see he put a lot of work into it, but I had no idea what it all added up to."

"What did it have to do with us? It wasn't relevant; I felt like this person was just wasting our time."

"I didn't feel the speaker cared about the subject——or me."

"There was too much repetition."

You've probably felt that way yourself. Knowing how sleepy most audiences get, you may tighten up just thinking about writing a speech for them. But don't comfort yourself, as you prepare, with pride in your dignity——you can be so dignified you sound like a statue on a snowy day. Or your expertise—— you can be such an expert that no one understands more than a sentence or two. Or your extemporaneity——you can do it so off the cuff that your speech has no order, no suspense, no message.

Instead of adopting an attitude, you should begin by thinking of your opening gesture, even if you're planning a brief sit-down report before a circle of colleagues. A short speech is a speech; an informal "talk"——open to questions, ready for give and take——is still formal enough to require preparation. You need to think out your message, then look at that message as if you were an actor. As the speaker, you are the star in a small drama. So do what an actor would.

Get Their Attention—Right Off

Make your audience like you——or admit they don't. Show why they should care about you or your subject. Give them half a dozen reasons why they should bother to listen:

- What's essential to them? And how does your topic relate to that?
- Why are they here now? How can your speech help them?
- What do you have in common with them?

- As far as they are concerned, who are you? What do they expect from you? How can you go beyond that role?
- Does your speech concern an issue that has divided this audience? Will you be rekindling old feuds, encouraging them to take sides again, or showing them how to resolve their differences?
- What economic motive do they have for listening? Intellectual? Emotional?

Develop One Main Idea

Audiences want to be moved. They do not want someone standing there mumbling about half a dozen unrelated facts. They want someone to take a clear position and defend it.

A central idea offers the audience a way of organizing what they hear, anticipating what you will say, spotting the intelligence behind the flow of facts and phrases. An idea gives them something to take home. An idea can change their minds.

If you feel you have nothing to say to this audience, you may be assuming they know more than you do about just about everything: so look for small areas that you care about:

- What could your group, division, industry do better? What irritates you about current practices?
- What problems does your group face, and what solutions do you favor?
- What changes do you foresee?
- What events led up to a new policy, and how will the policy work?
- What inconsistencies do you see in current thinking? How could you resolve these?

I *don't* recommend a blow-by-blow recounting of every last thing you did on a project. (You make the audience count the minutes to the present.) Or a series of thoughts, not related to each other, on a number of topics. (If they don't fit together, why put them in the same speech? Audiences keep trying to make a message out of all this unrelated stuff—and that's frustrating.) Or speaking on something you don't care about. (Emotion carries the audience. Indifference makes you look like a bloodless snob.) Or the same thing you talked about last year. (Maybe it worked fine then, but this year you're different; the situation has changed; the same words may sound sour now.)

Whatever topic you end up with, make a sentence out of it. For instance, if you choose to talk about production methods in general, you have too much to discuss. To limit the talk, and make it mean something, focus on a particular recommendation, or conclusion.

NOT JUST A TOPIC, AN IDEA

NOT JUST A TOPIC,	AN IDEA
Production methods	We should decentralize our production, so that each division can set its own priorities and control its own schedule.
Promotion accounting	We must insist on proof of promotion within 90 days of the ad's appearance, with notarized bills, before we pay our share on co-op ads. Otherwise, we'll go on being ripped off.
Length of sales calls	Our reps must rehearse giving the key facts about a new product in less than five minutes. Our customers manage stores, and if we talk too long, we both lose business. They get mad, and we skedaddle—without a sale.

The key to a convincing speech is to believe it. That means you must build on an idea that you understand thoroughly yourself—not just in your mind but in your guts. You must care. If you don't, find a different theme.

Define What You Want the Audience to Do

What do you want them to do after your speech? Vote right? Shout? Change their production methods? Keep that image in your mind as you draft your speech. Lead up to it. Explain how to do it. Draw pictures. Give aerial views. Whatever it takes, rehearse that action for the audience, so that they get used to it, and can remember it.

Memory is odd. A day after the average speech, most people have only a vague memory of the person who gave it, and a one-sentence recall of the idea. A week or so later, even the topic fades.

Your job is to get remembered. Like a ski instructor teaching a new turn, you've got to encourage the audience to imagine the action—done correctly—several times, during your speech, before they'll begin thinking that they could do it too.

Some people learn more by hearing, some by seeing, some by doing. Appeal to each learning style. Show slides, diagrams, or models; run films or TV; hand out objects and have people manipulate them the way you want. Create a three-dimensional speech, if you can.

Calculate Your Visual Effects Beforehand

Since they are so important, plan your visuals early. For each key point, a visual expression. And that image should express only one idea—not more.

Most people cram too much into each slide. If it's a graph, they put six lines in, intersecting in a crazy-quilt pattern. Restrain yourself. Show one line, then another, then another. If you must sum up the intersections, do that only after you've shown them individually.

On each slide or chart, make the symbols big and clear—nothing too sophisticated. Fine lines fade for the people in the back row. Put an identifying sentence on each one—a whole idea, not just a topic. And repeat that sentence on your handout, so the audience can keep track.

Where possible, throw in faces. People like to see people more than charts. Use colors to distinguish ideas. Tests suggest that the most legible combinations of colors are black on yellow, blue on yellow, green on white, and red on white.

Test out your order of presentation, too. Rehearse your speech three or four times with the images, and ask yourself:

- Does one image lead easily into the next?
- Do you provide all the simple versions before a complicated summary?
- Do you repeat any images unnecessarily?
- Do you provide signpost slides, indicating that you are leaving one major section in your speech, and embarking on another? (These should also echo your handout.)
- Does one topic change color in the middle? Maybe people have gotten used to seeing the Midwest sales figures in red, but for some reason, halfway through, red begins to stand for European sales. This way lies confusion.

During your speech, read what's on the slides. Don't feel compelled to improvise in order to avoid repeating yourself. Repeat yourself. That way the audience knows you are talking about this slide—not some other subject that comes before or after.

In general, avoid overhead projectors. Those pale images of typed pages tell more about the wall they're on than the speech you're giving. If you want people to read type, give them photocopies.

Give the Audience a Lot of Paper

You can reinforce your logic with a multi-page handout, too. At the very least, prepare a list of the subjects you'll cover, in order. Even better is an outline of the ideas you'll be presenting.

Pass that out at the beginning. This is not a take-home assignment. It is a way to help people understand your speech. Design your handouts so your listeners can see how they correspond to your main ideas. That way, when reading through it, they'll get a preview of what you think, so they can relate what you're talking about now with an overall theme. Some people like to jump ahead, to get a sense of your whole speech, then come back and listen, seeing how what you say ties in to that main point. Others follow with their finger, so they never miss anything. Still others pay no attention for ten minutes, then use the outline to find out where you are. For many, reading what they hear makes the point sink in.

If you're planning to show a number of slides, make sure that the text on the slides agrees with the text on your handout, so everyone knows just where you are. Inconsistency makes people wonder if they're lost, or if there's any significance in the odd disparity between the two phrasings.

Be complete. If you've got a technical audience, include all the details; when talking to a professional group, write your speech out well ahead of time, then get it photocopied, so everyone can have a copy. If you're talking to a general audience, just outline the highlights. But do outline.

Plan Activities

Sitting still for an hour gives people a backache. When your presentation risks running longer than half an hour, add some physical activities, some discussions. Let them get up and stretch, move around, act out a part, talk with their neighbors.

These activities get their blood moving, and that may wake up their brains.

The advantages are that you let people rehearse the actions you want them to do later. You let them imagine a situation more thoroughly, so they can see why you'd recommend what you do. You give them a break.

When you decide to stop your speech and get the audience actively involved, ask yourself these questions:

- Have I advertised my point before, during, and after the exercise?
- Will people really see that this activity demonstrates this main idea?
- Have I tried this exercise out on small groups, to make sure people do what I expect?
- Have I prepared a chart and a handout explaining exactly what I want people to do?
- If the activity requires that different people do different things, have I given them separate orders?
- Have I gotten all the necessary props, papers, pens, and costumes?
- Have I arranged the room, chairs, tables so people can do the exercise?

Anticipate Questions and Arguments

You've attended meetings where the speaker asks for questions, and can't answer them—or gets none, and stands there in embarrassed silence. So anticipate the worst questions you could get, and draft answers. You may never use them, but you'll feel calmer when you open the floor up to questions.

To make sure you get questions, you might close your speech with some suggestions:

Now I know some of you may have questions like these: "How in hell are we going to do this?" "When is all this going to happen?" and "Who exactly could do this?" I've sketched out the answers to them in general terms; but if you'd like more details, just ask.

You can also set up your whole speech as a request for opinions. You could start by saying you need their advice, then show what you think the situation requires and ask what they think. The earlier you make a call for their ideas, the longer they have to think—so more people will have questions.

Prepare, Test, Rehearse

Some people like to talk from notes, others from a complete text. Either way is fine.

You certainly don't *have to* write out every word. Having a complete text can sometimes make you feel hobbled, a little like a high school student in speech class. For some meetings, you have to provide a written-out version for the audience. But that doesn't mean you have to stick to it word for word. Do follow the outline, though.

If you prefer notes, put your key ideas in short sentences. That way, if you lose your place or forget what the point is, you can just read something, and it will make sense—a lot more sense than a topic alone.

NOT JUST PHRASES,	*WHOLE IDEAS*
Preparations	We need $100,000 and a staff of three for a three-month preparatory study.
Tax status	Our accountants report that this company's tax status is unclear because of recent IRS rulings.

If possible, rehearse your whole speech—with handouts and visuals—before a group of people you can count on to give you real criticism. Ask them to answer these questions: does the order make sense? Which parts seemed repetitious? What would they cut? Add?

Keep the focus on organization. It's too easy for people to get bogged down in the details of one slide, and leave you with no advice about the overall shape of your speech. But your audience usually cares about general significance—not the little squiggles in the corner of one picture.

In fact, whenever you get nervous about the speech you're about to give, you can calm down by thinking about your main point—what you want to get across. If you focus on that, you'll give a great speech, even if you leave out a whole section or fluff the boss's name.

||||||||||||||||||||||||||||||||||||||||||||||||||||||||||||||||||||||||||||||||||||||||||||||

If you lose all your notes on the way to the podium, talk from your summary. Here's mine:

- Get their attention—right off.
- Develop one main idea.
- Define what you want the audience to do.
- Calculate your visual effects beforehand.
- Give the audience a lot of paper.
- Plan activities.
- Anticipate questions and arguments.
- Prepare, test, rehearse.

□ FORMS □

|||||||||||||||||||||||||||||||||||||||||||||||||||||||||||||||||||||||||||||||||

This is how most forms get drawn up—blindfolded. Boxes go here, labels somewhere up there. Key information ends up buried in the middle, or left out altogether, while unimportant data floats to the top. There's often no room on the form to write your full name.

If you want to make up a new form, think about the ones you've hated in the past. Ask yourself:

- Who needs this information?
- Am I just making more work for people?
- What's wrong with having no form at all? Can you quantify the cost?

When you start, you may find many people on your staff want a form, but no one quite knows what should be on it. Probe for decisions:

- What decisions depend on the information in this form?
- How much does it cost you when one of these decisions goes wrong because of misinformation?
- What facts do these decisions hinge on?
- What other facts can be ignored?
- If disaster strikes, what facts do you need to make a quick patch?
- In what areas do you need some extra space for exceptions, special cases, sad stories?
- Can you streamline the form, and avoid confusion from bad handwriting, by turning a form with questions into a checklist?

Then you might go to the people who will have to fill out the form and ask *them* questions:

- Which of these facts come easily to mind, and can be written down without difficulty or error?
- What order do they naturally arrange these facts in? (How does this correspond to the order in which your staff wants to read the facts off the form?)
- Which facts fit into the same amount of space every time? Which vary tremendously?
- Which responses seem hard to recall or look up? (Does your staff really need these? Can your staff stand the inevitable errors in this area?)

- Where would these people like extra space for comments? And what would they like you to leave off?

Group items so they make sense to the people who have to fill the form in. Follow their way of thinking, associations, sequences. If that familiar order conflicts with the way your staff wants to read the items, so be it. When you only fill out one form a month, you may get confused fast, and make a mess of key questions, but when you're reading a hundred forms, you learn pretty quickly to spot the data you need, no matter where it ends up.

The more you ask people what they think of your first draft, the more drafts you'll do. But the form will get better—easier to fill out, more helpful to the readers, faster to process. If you have the time and patience, try out each version of the form for a few months, then go back and ask people how it's working. You'll find what you left out, what drives people crazy, what can be dropped, and whether you would combine this form with others.

As you revise, see what you can do to improve readability.

- Do your instructions point to the right slots, or do they hover vaguely in between several boxes?
- Can you read the labels without a magnifying glass?
- Have you kept your captions and labels consistent throughout?
- Have you eliminated lines, rules, and boxes wherever possible? (Small boxes make for cramped handwriting; many boxes guarantee confusion).
- Have you put unimportant information, such as the form's number and your company logo, down at the bottom on the left?
- Have you put borders around key boxes?
- Have you put boxes for totals and results down at the bottom, on the right, where most people expect them?

- Do you have wide left margins for forms that will end up in ring binders?

You can make your forms easier to fill out.

- Reduce the number of tab stops, so a typist can set the tabs once and fill out all lines, rather than jimmying the paper around every which way just to add the next fact.
- Use check boxes where possible, to keep people from scribbling. Ask for "x's", not checks, too. An "x" centers on the box; a check can sprawl over several boxes, leaving your staff unsure which box was meant.
- If the form gets filled out by staff while they're standing, make all boxes bigger.

Forms multiply. One form often comes out in quadruplicate or worse. Try to put some limits on this proliferation. For instance, if five people want separate copies of the same form, make sure they really need them all at the same time if they really need the form at all. Couldn't they just pass the same form along? Are they responsible for something documented here, or are they just collecting paper? If all five people must have copies, assign the same number to all five sheets, then distinguish the sheets by color. If there's an area one person wants to keep everyone else out of, shade it on the other copies, and leave it clear on his.

The best form is none at all. The second best is the one you don't have to write anything on, just enter a few marks. The worst is an income tax form. That's one we'd all rather not look at. Keep it in mind as a model of what to avoid.

□ *DIRECT MAIL* □

||||||||||||||||||||||||||||||||||||||||||||||||||||||||||||||||||||||||||||||

When you write an ad and send it directly to your customer, when you announce a new service center or solicit charitable donations for your local United Fund, you may think of yourself as a Rough Rider ballyhooing into people's houses and shouting your news. But the customer thinks of you as junk mail.

Too many solicitations for funds, too many catalogs, too many subscription pitches, too many insurance offers—that's what you're up against. Most people are standing up when they glance at your letter—not a posture that encourages a leisurely read. If they are at work, your letter seems like a distraction; if they are at home after work, your letter may be seen as a salesman breaking into their privacy. That's why so many people boast that they chuck letters like yours.

And even when customers actually read the letter, they tend to react this way:

> "It's not for me. I don't know anyone who would want stuff like that." (Oops, wrong mailing list!)
> "I couldn't figure out what they were trying to sell, so I just threw it away." (Usually you have less than a minute to convince them to read on.)
> "They hid the price so much, I gave up trying to find it, and put the letter away. I don't know where." (Why make it hard to buy?)
> "There wasn't any reply card, and I couldn't find the address, so I figured they weren't too efficient as a company." (You forgot them, again.)

You can avoid most of these mishaps if you respect the work you're doing. A lot of newcomers to this corner of the ad business sneer at other people's efforts, and ignore what can be learned. That's odd, because this is one type of writing in which you can measure your results in dollars: you can see that one letter brought ten times as much money as another. But if you don't test out different possibilities, and don't bother to study the research that's already been done, you're likely to repeat the blunders a thousand other people have made before.

Here are a few tips to help you get started.

Make Clear Exactly Whom You're Talking To

Don't use one letter to appeal to teenagers with acne, grandparents, farmers, city bus drivers, new mothers, and welders. Only the Sears catalog can do that.

Pick out one audience, and tell them you're talking to them. Yes, you'll discourage some people from reading your letter. But you'll interest the ones who really count—the people who are most likely to buy your product.

Incidentally, the same principle applies to fund raising. You have a product here, too—a little less tangible, perhaps, but still a product. The feeling of pride that comes from identifying with a good cause; the joy of generosity; the comfort of a well-fed vanity. And you're going to want to match your mailing list carefully with the kind of appeal you choose.

You're "qualifying" the prospect. You don't waste postage on people who might read your whole letter with interest—and then realize they just don't need your product. And you catch the eye of the people you really have to reach, the ones who need or want just what you're offering.

So be as specific as you can. If possible, name your audience in your headlines:

- Announcing a new insurance plan for men under 35! Because you're young, you earn interest on every penny.
- Now your safe driving record entitles you to a 15% discount on auto insurance!
- Are you a big woman? You'll love our extra-large fashions.

Notice that you're making these people some kind of promise. So make one that will appeal to them—not actors or gardeners or other groups.

Know What You're Promising

You need to immerse yourself in all the details of your product, then look at them from the point of view of this particular audience, to see which ones will have the greatest appeal. Figure out what the key benefit will be—for them.

- What is the main reason people will tell themselves they are buying your product, and not someone else's?
- What is the strongest emotional reason they will choose your product over someone else's?

To discover these reasons, talk with sales people, customers, research people. Interrogate yourself—if you're part of the target audience. Recognize that the practical reason alone will not drive people to buy. What's your best emotional promise?

You'll probably come up with a dozen benefits, on your first pass. Keep looking. You should have at least fifty on your list.

One way to turn up new ones is to study your product as if you'd never seen it before. Pick it apart. Consult with every expert in the firm. Peer into every nook and cranny, nut, bolt, and screw. What's it made out of? What makes it unique? Why is your company unique? What do customers say about every part of the product?

What you're discovering, along with the potential benefits, are the details that make your promises convincing. Incidentally, those will also help you fill up your pages. David Ogilvy, the ad man, says that his company's research shows that long letters outsell short ones.

Start Selling Right Away

Right on the envelope, you can start selling—or turn a lot of people off. Think about the mail you trash without opening. What are the factors that signal you that this envelope won't interest you?

The worst envelope copy is just a return address. A real name over the address is better, particularly if it's a signature. Still better is a design, and an appeal aimed at the audience's self-interest.

For instance, your typeface, paper quality, and phrasing can suggest that you're an upper-class club, offering culture to those who can afford the unnecessary extra yacht. Or that you're a bargain basement, brimming with marked-down brand-name items, ready to ship.

The most successful mailings cover the envelope with phrases that will tease my curiosity, greed, lust—whatever will eventually motivate me to fill out your coupon. Examples:

- You may already have won . . .
- Special offer—for our best customers!
- Advance notice.
- You could double your income in a year, using the system we describe in this important bulletin.

Write a Lot of Long Headlines

Put every benefit in its own long headline. Yes, long. Research suggests that lengthy headlines catch people's attention and keep them reading, unlike long paragraphs.

Here are some ideas for headlines:

- Put money right up there. How much does your product cost? (Yes, don't hide that.) How much does it save? How much is this offer, campaign, lottery worth?
- Use dates. That increases the urgency.
- Include names: your name, the boss's name, the company name, the product. If they're famous, the names will sell; if not, they'll *look* famous.
- Quote someone giving a testimonial. Tests show that people are able to recall headlines like this better than most.
- Make up some newspaper headlines, as if you were announcing something really new.
- Key your announcements to holidays, seasons, special

events. That gives the customer a reason to buy now—not later.

- Stress speed. Use words like "fast," "quick," "instant," "ready to go."
- Look at the headlines that keep appearing over and over in ads and direct mail letters that you're familiar with. They probably work. (When you find a headline that works, use it again. There's no prize for originality in direct mail.)

Rewrite each headline at least half a dozen times to bring out the exact promise your audience wants to hear. But don't try combining too many benefits in one headline. Instead, shuffle the headlines around, to see how they work in sequences.

After a while, you'll begin to see which one's going to be your lead and which ones will work as subheads. Before you worry about the text, organize the sequence of headlines so they lead up to your coupon.

Make Your Text Rewarding

The copy that follows each headline must arouse the customers' imaginations, reassure their consciences, confirm their hopes. In general, that means that you should stress the satisfaction not the work or costs that may be involved.

Give the details behind your headlines. Break down money figures. Quote authorities at length.

Tell stories, if you can. Stress examples of people who have had great success using your product, people who made a name for themselves by contributing to your cause, people who helped save a little kid or an endangered species, just by sending five dollars to your organization.

The stories that work best in commercials will probably work best here, such as a problem, then a solution using your product, of course. Or a cynic who learns that your product really is terrific, after all. Or a real-life down-home just-folks testimonial to the virtues of your product.

Make sure your promises are believable. You will reassure me if you qualify your grander gestures with some disclaimers. Admit what your product won't do. Include any details that make me see that your company is reliable, reputable, and rich. I want to know you'll be around to service my gizmo when it breaks; that you stand behind your guarantees.

Finally, mention the name of your product over and over. Remember, the customers don't know it as well as you do. Repetition helps them remember.

Make Your Pictures Tell a Story

If you can afford pictures, use them. Show somebody using your product, or illustrate the rewards of having bought your product.

These images help people imagine they're in the picture. The more they think about using your product, the more they are likely to buy it. Basically, a picture can do everything that text can, reinforcing the message, livening up the page, catching the browser's eye.

Keep Readers Active

Tests indicate that the more someone actually does with your letter, the more likely that person is to buy the product. That's why the big sweepstakes letters seem like party games. You can spend most of an afternoon with activities like this: cutting out the bonus circles and pasting them on the giant coupon; tearing off the individual prize numbers, so you'll have them when the money truck arrives; ripping apart the magazine stickers, and pasting four of them on the reply coupon; picking one of the two envelopes (the yes or the no); sorting through the pink warning about mailing today, the green appeal not to turn down the offer, the four-color eight-page fold-out outlining the prizes; punching out an additional bonus prize symbol and fitting that into a cut-out slot on the coupon; circling the secret code on the coupon to get the extra extra-bonus.

After doing all this, it seems simple to order four magazines you don't really want. After all, it's the least you can do for them, now that they're going to make you a millionaire. (Only the strong resist this impulse.)

You know the old salesman's trick of getting you to say yes to half a dozen innocuous questions, so you'll be ready to say yes to a five-year contract. Well, giving the reader lots of activities can work the same way.

Define Your Offer

This can be the hardest writing you face: spelling out exactly what you are offering, and designing the coupon and the main text so that anyone can understand what you are promising.

Offer four or five different alternatives—from the cheapest to the most expensive. Persuade me to commit myself to more than I intended. Define exactly what I get in each category, and show me why each one is a bargain.

Point out that my neighbors are paying more to another company. Convince me that you have in fact lowered your price, or added a lot of value for the old price. Give me some way of measuring how much of a deal I'm getting.

In fact, give me some rationale for your low, low price. For instance, you got a bargain yourself. You're clearing out inventory. You want to sign up new customers fast. Whatever. But the better the explanation, the more I'll believe I'm actually getting a discount.

If possible, give me something, too. A free bumper sticker.

A founding membership. A guarantee. A chance to get my money back if I don't like the product.

Make It a Snap to Order

If I put your coupon aside until tomorrow, I probably won't fill it out. If I can't find the coupon, I'll give up. So, make your coupon stand out. Don't hide it—feature it.

Give it enough room to include your complete offer, plus your address and phone number. (Too many people leave their address off, forcing readers to comb through the rest of the letter for someplace to send the coupon.) And leave enough space for clumsy hand lettering. Don't leave the reader feeling like a fool, trying to fit the address into a one-inch slot.

And make sure they know why they should send in your coupon *today*. Perhaps you only have a limited supply or the price reduction is temporary. Perhaps this is a special market test or a one-time-only offer. Or maybe you give an even better deal as a bonus for promptness.

So When You're Writing Directly to a Potential Customer . . .

- Make clear exactly whom you're talking to.
- Know what you're promising.
- Start selling right away.
- Write a lot of long headlines.
- Make your text rewarding.
- Make your pictures tell a story.
- Keep readers active.
- Define your offer.
- Make it a snap to order.

□ *PROCEDURES* □

To carry out a policy, we often need step-by-step instructions or written procedures. You may end up writing these when you're managing a group, analyzing work flow, setting up a new system, or trouble-shooting an old one.

When you write procedures clearly, new workers can find out how to do their jobs and how they fit into the business without fumbling for months. The whole staff can turn to your procedures to resolve questions such as:

- Where do I start?
- What's happened so far?
- Whom do I give the completed forms to?
- What happens then?

- Do I have a deadline?
- Will I get any feedback?
- Do I have anything else I have to do later?
- How do I know I'm done?

Most procedures baffle understanding. Here's a sample of comments workers have made about procedures:

"Those Standard Operating Procedures use too many big words."

"This procedure refers outside too often. And it's too hard to find the stuff it refers to."

"I can never find the exact step I'm working on."

"Too much talk."

"Whoever wrote that doesn't know what we really do down here."

"They use computer jargon, and that doesn't mean anything out here in the warehouse."

"They don't go through things in order."

The usual conclusion is that most "Standard Practices" are unreadable. As a result, few employees comply with the policy. Confusion continues, tinged now with resentment at having been teased with an explanation that does not explain.

Talk to the People Who Do the Work

The first step toward writing understandable procedures takes you out of your office. Ask the person who's involved: what do you normally do first? And then what? And who does the next step?

Find out what usually happens, and how the new policy really will change that. Stress the *usual*—subordinate the occasional variation or exception. Discover the routine.

You'll probably learn a lot about each person's job. Since

your aim is to give everyone a picture of the whole process, outline the main steps each person takes, but leave the minor details for later.

As you write, check back with each person, get their suggestions, revise the procedure, and check back again. You may discover that no one really knows who's responsible for a particular step; you may have to call a head-to-head meeting to resolve who really does what here. Or you may notice that one person seems to appear and disappear five or six times in a routine. Maybe his activity could be done all at once. Thus, as you talk, and write, and talk again, you will be clarifying and simplifying the actual procedure.

Define Your Subject

Keep in mind that a procedure acts as a road map through the company, a flow chart of work on a particular project. So don't get sidetracked. Pursue the project even when it moves through one department after another, like this:

Plant Foreman
1. Fills out Form 132, "Requisition," describing needed machinery.
2. Sends completed Form 132 to Purchasing Clerk.

Purchasing Clerk
3. Checks with suppliers for estimated costs.
4. Makes sure plant budget can meet costs.
5. Orders from cheapest source.

Warehouse Clerk
6. Receives shipment.
7. Uses Form 31B to notify Plant Foreman and Purchasing Clerk that shipment has arrived.

If the procedure seems to be getting too long, divide it into sections, phases, or stages. But be clear about what actions start and close out a phase, so the reader can move easily from one to the next. For instance, you might slice up parts of Personnel Procedures this way:

- From placing want ad to employee's starting day in "Hiring Procedures"
- From updating staff budget to employee's receipt of the raise, in "Wage Procedures"
- From firing to sealing of employee's file in "Termination Procedures"

Exclude the Background

Many "Standard Procedure" bulletins postpone the actual procedure for half a page or more with unnecessary background like all the dates of previous publications, definitions before we know why we should care about the terms, statements of lofty purpose, and cheerful slogans and pep talks.

File all that. You need it to prepare for writing, but don't make the reader thumb through it.

The worst offense contained in most procedures is that policy statements keep creeping in. Yes, they *are* relevant. After all, the procedure shows people how to carry out the policy. But to learn how to order replacement parts for the copier, a clerk doesn't need to read:

> In order to maintain profitability and clear accountability, it shall henceforth be the declared policy of this Company, and all its subsidiaries and divisions, to require thorough investigations, needs assessments, feasibility studies, or other necessary research, followed by competitive bidding on all purchases, the responsibility for said studies to lie with the Originating Department and the Purchasing Department.
>
> —A Fortune 500 company

Sure, but what form do I fill out? Whom do I call?

Digest the policy, and make sure it really is reflected in the procedure. But most of all, focus on actions. Remember, the reader is asking you: "What am I supposed to do?"

Look for the Starting Point—And Outcome

As you discuss the procedure with different people, you may find yourself pondering its exact limits. Where does this procedure begin? Look for an action that sets the rest of the procedure in motion:

- A driver has an accident. (Insurance Procedures)
- A customer places an order. (Sales Procedures)
- An engineer suggests a change. (Design Procedures)

Avoid broad philosophic openers like this: "When the purchasing process has begun, the buyer must maintain and update the Purchase Log at regular intervals." How can the employee tell that this mysterious "process" has begun? He or she must be able to tell the light's turned green. An action happens—or does not. Someone does it—or doesn't. That's why you should use an action to prompt the next person in the chain.

At the end of the procedure describe the particular action that closes out the process.

- The insurance company check arrives and is deposited.
- The customer receives order.
- The engineer's change is actually made.

In this way we define where the procedure starts and stops. In between, we track the most common activities.

Follow the Routine

If 80 percent of a project's transactions take place one way, follow that line of action. The ordinary is what we're after.

Don't omit the exceptions, but subordinate them. If certain information applies only to one person, cut that out. He or she may need more instruction to carry out the part (if so, create personal procedures), but the others reading this don't need to plow through those details.

Stick to the main road, so each person can see: (1) how the procedure usually goes; and (2) where he or she fits into the whole.

Work Step by Step

Number every step of the procedure as you go, so employees can tell where they come into the overall process. Don't start the numbering over for each person; instead, show where their job falls in the continuum.

Most procedures can be described in less than two dozen steps. But don't try to meet some predetermined number. In fact, keep looking for missing or "hidden" steps. Let all the steps emerge.

Say Who Does What

So employees can locate their own work fast, identify clearly who performs each step. Put job titles off to the left, floating in enough white space so they're easy to spot. You might head this lefthand column "Who" or "Person Responsible."

Use job titles rather than names, because individuals come and go, and you can't count on a new employee learning people's names that fast. Whenever possible, avoid making a whole department responsible for filling out a form. There must be a particular individual who usually does that.

In the righthand column, lead off with an active verb saying what the person does. Not "is responsible for," but "terminates." Not "in these circumstances," but "schedules." Starting with a verb forces you to describe a real action, rather than a situation. We know the situation; we want to know what to do about it.

And while you're at it, trim the long words.

INSTEAD OF:	SAY:
ascertain	find out
distribute	send
establish	set up
provide	give

If you look at each step from left to right, then, you'll see it answers the question, "Who does what when in the sequence?"

Stock Clerk	31. Receives item.
	32. Logs item in.
	33. Turns over to mailroom.
Mail Clerk	34. Delivers to department.

Avoid Detours

In general, keep your eye on the usual. But when you encounter exceptions to the rule, indent them as subsets of the main activity. Sometimes you'll just refer the problem to someone who can make a case-by-case decision:

Checkout Clerk	21. If name is not on Bad Check list, initial the check.
	21a. If name *is* on Bad Check list, give check to Floor Supervisor.

Floor Supervisor	21b. Call up Customer Records, and determine how many times customer has written us checks against insufficient funds.
	21c. If more than 3 times, refuse to honor check.
	21d. If less than 3 times, note that on check, and return to Checkout Clerk for cashing.
Checkout Clerk	22. Enter amount, and press Check Key.

Or you may want to refer the reader to another procedure, to handle just this problem.

Receiving Clerk	12. Inspects to see if product is damaged.
	12a. If so, starts Damage Reporting Procedure.
	12b. If not, enters "OK" on Form 115.
	13. Sends out copies of Form 115 as follows:
	13a. White copy to Accounts Payable Clerk.
	13b. Pink copy to Requesting Officer.
	13c. Green copy to Warehouse Clerk.

Show briefly what to do, whom to go to—or what other procedures to invoke. But don't get bogged down in these asides.

Detach Personal Procedures

If you find that one person performs a dozen steps at one time, see if you can summarize them in the company-wide procedure as "cleans up workspace." Then you can detail exactly what this person does in a separate "Cleaning Procedures" just for him.

Personal procedures look like systems procedures—they just don't involve so many people. They guide one person through one aspect of the job.

Cleaning Procedures

PERSON RESPONSIBLE	ACTION
Carpenter's Helper	1. Picks up usable wood, returns to shelves.
	2. Returns tools to marked locations.
	3. Collects loose nails, screws, and other hardware; puts in appropriate cans.
	4. Throws chunks, butt ends, and other debris into trash bin.
	5. Dusts surfaces of saws, file cabinets, window ledges.
	6. Removes industrial vacuum cleaner from closet.
	7. Attaches wide nozzle.
	8. Vacuums floor and surfaces.
	9. Empties vacuum bag in trash bin.
	10. Installs new vacuum bag.
	11. Returns vacuum to closet.
	12. Cleans all windows.

Revising Old Procedures

You may have to update procedures that read like this one (from a county hospital in California):

> It is the Personnel Clerk's responsibility to place all completed applications in the most appropriate Position File immediately upon receipt of completed application from applicant, including said Personnel Clerk's annotations as to applicant's willingness to follow instructions to complete said multi-copy form, applicant's possible abuse of a dangerous controlled substance, applicant's general demeanor, and other pertinent observations on applicant's appearance and behavior.

After you've talked to the Personnel Clerk to find out what that means, you might rewrite the procedures taking the step-by-step approach. At first you may feel you're just putting down the obvious, but soon you'll enter areas where the clerk didn't know what he or she was supposed to do. Have patience—you're sorting things out.

Applicant	1. Enters, asks for application.
Personnel Clerk	2. Asks what position applicant is interested in.
	3. Hands out application and a ball-point pen, urging applicant to press firmly when writing.
	3a. Points out where to fill in Position Sought.
	3b. Shows where to put Previous Employment.
	3c. Shows where to sign.
Applicant	4. Asks questions about form.
Personnel Clerk	5. Answers.

Applicant	6. Hands in form.
Personnel Clerk	7. Looks over to make sure all slots are filled in.

       7a. If not, asks applicant to finish filling in form.

       7b. Notes if applicant refuses.

       7c. If form is completed, thanks applicant, and explains Call-Back Procedure.

    8. Notes if applicant showed signs of drug abuse.

    9. Grades personal appearance and courtesy.

       9a. A means excellent.

       9b. B means good.

       9c. C means poor or worse.

   10. Reports any other impressions of applicant.

   11. Files application under Position Sought in Applications File.

Why the Step-by-Step Method Helps

As you write these step-by-step procedures, you will bring to light certain gaps, repetitions, and inconsistencies in current or proposed procedures. And you may force *someone* to take responsibility for acting in areas no one wants to touch. So the process of writing clarifies the procedures. And because you have to keep checking back with people, they will see what you're asking them to do. So there will be less resistance when you finally ask their approval of the new procedures. (Many approvals get delayed because the manager doesn't understand what he's being asked to sign.)

As a result of the step-by-step method, you make it easy for an employee to find where he or she takes part in the procedure; how he or she should perform a particular task; and who is responsible for other steps.

What to Do

Here is a summary of this chapter in step-by-step procedure form.

Procedure for Writing Procedures

WHO	DOES WHAT
Writer	1. Reads all background material, including policy statements, earlier procedures.
	2. Arranges interviews with employees involved.
	3. Asks employees exactly what they do, and in what order.
Each Employee	4. Explains each step.
Writer	5. Writes up what each does.
	6. Shows that to each employee.
Each Employee	7. Corrects, refines description.
Writer	8. Repeats Steps 5–7 until employee agrees with description.
	9. Excludes background data.
	10. Looks for the starting point— and outcome—of the whole procedure.
	11. Follows the routine.
	12. Works step by step.

12a. Numbers consecutively
throughout procedure.

12b. If numbers go much above
24, considers dividing material into different phases.

13. Says who does what. (Uses job
titles.)

14. Avoids detours.

15. Detaches personal procedures.

16. Secures approvals.

17. Distributes.

□ *TRAINING MATERIALS* □

You may be facing a problem that memos can't solve.
Has production fallen off? Are people losing their
motivation? Do you have to show them a new way of working
or a new machine?

If so, you may decide to create a little course for them. But
remember what happened in some of the training sessions
you've been to. You've probably had reactions like these

(taken from evaluations of a course at a Fortune 500 manufacturer):

"It was boring."

"I couldn't see any reason why we had to go."

"How does this apply? How am I supposed to use this on the job?"

"I liked having the morning off. But now I have a big pile of memos and phone messages sitting on my desk."

"I thought I got the idea when I was sitting there, but when I got back to the machine, I couldn't remember a thing."

As one frustrated trainer said, "I trained them, but they didn't learn."

Most training fails during the planning and writing—long before the actual session begins. Common reasons for failure include:

- There was a problem to be solved, but training wasn't the way to do it.
- The objectives of the course were never clearly stated.
- The course taught last things first, and left out steps.
- Without any warm-up, people were plunged into a lengthy lecture, with no discussion or questions.
- No one got any practice.

You can avoid boring or confusing your audience by doing what trainers like to call "front-end analysis."

Analyze Before You Write

Study the problem in detail to find out exactly what's going on now, and how you want to change that. Here are some questions you might ask at this stage:

- What behavior needs to be changed?
- Whose behavior are we talking about? (Is it everyone in the group? New employees? People in Section Three?)
- Who else is involved? (Supervisors, contacts.)
- What causes the problem now?
- Exactly what should people be doing, after training? (You should be able to specify the step-by-step procedures people will be able to follow after they've been through your training program.)
- How does current behavior differ from that ideal?

Define Your Objectives

At the beginning of the course, write down what you want people to be able to do when they're through. Actions, not feelings. Behavior you can measure. If you want, you can refine this even more, by specifying exactly how you'll measure their performance. It's not enough for people to end up "knowing" or "thinking" something. They should be able to do something you can see. Leave appreciation for courses in music.

This is a description of the contents of a course:

> This course will examine the history of the X-23, previous models, current enhancements, and operator input.

Here is a statement of objectives:

> After this course, you will be able to operate the X-23 so well you can produce 50 units an hour.

State the objective right at the start of the course. When people know what they're supposed to learn, they learn it better.

Get It in Order

Figure out what people need to know first. Then what? And then what? In this way you create a table of contents for your course, a list of the main topics you'll cover. Each topic deserves its own lesson. (The outline of the whole course should be presented to students in the first hour, so they understand how each lesson relates to the main objective.)

One of the most confusing courses I've ever taken started without any announcement as to the point of the course, and without any schedule. The instructor just began talking about exceptions only an expert would care about, jumped to a few fine points about purchase orders, then ambled back to the reasons someone might want to buy, mentioning delivery problems along the way. People in the class got whiplash, watching the ideas zip back and forth.

If everyone in your class acknowledges there is a problem, bring that up first, then talk solutions. Say "why" before "how." Stress principles before details. Otherwise, you may find yourself moving backward as you realize that before you discuss "B," you must make "A" clear.

As you organize your topics, follow the most natural sequence. For example, show the class how to turn the machine on before you get into using it. Getting your topics in a logical order will help people understand how one flows into another. Students will make more connections, remember more.

And make sure you're not leaving out steps. (This is easy to do. You can forget some key step, assuming people know that when they don't.)

In planning the sequence of topics, you should also be getting a sense of the time needed to explain them all. If you have not taught or done training before, you'll probably wildly underestimate the time you need. It is not enough to say something once when training. You'll need to have people think about it, discuss it, try it out physically, review the process, and maybe even try it again and review it again——if you really want them to remember it.

The more your training involves changing habitual ways of thinking or feeling, the longer it will take. And the more you'll need to use a variety of training techniques to make each idea sink in.

Use a Variety of Training Techniques

Some people learn mainly by hearing, some by seeing, others by doing. Some can handle words with grace; others have trouble describing their own room. Some can picture in their minds three-dimensional shapes revolving, others can't distinguish three shades of red. Some people get a lot out of talking with fellow workers; others prefer to sit alone and read. To reach people who have different ways of learning, you'll need a variety of training techniques.

You should plan to use all of these techniques in a training session:

- Warm-Ups
- Discussion
- Presentation
- Activities
- Testing

We'll look at each of these now.

Warm-Ups

When you start the training session, some people may be worried that they won't understand what you're talking about. Others fear being bored. Sometimes you're dealing with people who don't know each other, and hesitate to speak up among strangers. They may feel lonely, suspicious, doubtful.

You can help bring the group together by starting with an

amusing activity that forces them to talk to each other or work together.

Or you might ask a question and have people tell each other their answers. For instance, if you're going to be showing the class a new way of handling a series of forms, you might ask them to compile a list of all the problems they've had with the old forms. They could work in pairs to draw up lists, then pool their ideas—as you write them out on a flipchart up front.

Similarly, you could have people figure out what they want out of the training session. This helps you say "Yes, that's what we'll be talking about," or "No, we won't go into that." You may also discover topics you ought to add.

If you want to remind people of a problem they face on the job, you could have teams act out what happens when it comes up. Creating these skits forces people to give up being shy, because they have to improvise together and these brief dramas make everyone else laugh and applaud.

Try puzzles, guessing games, charades, team drawings. Get your class up and moving around, if possible. Be silly. People come to training sessions looking for relief from their regular job. Don't grade them, or force them into some competition that ends up with winners and losers.

Spend fifteen minutes, or not more than half an hour on a warm-up. Warm-ups sound unimportant, so lots of people leave them out of training sessions. But a well-designed warm-up can bring your people together, and set up a topic you're going to explore more seriously. Use a warm-up at the beginning of your course, and sometimes when you're about to launch a new topic. After lunch, you could call it a wake-up.

Lead a Discussion

It's tough figuring out how to start a real discussion, how to guide people through a series of general thoughts to a conclusion you want them to agree on.

First you have to know what *you* think. You have to trace the way you came to those conclusions. Perhaps you started thinking about a problem, tried out a few solutions, found those didn't work, and wondered what else might. Then you noticed a pattern that no one else had pointed out. Thinking about that led you to a question. As you thought about that, you saw a new solution emerging.

Your notes for the discussion might go like this:

- What's the problem?
- What solutions have we tried—and why have they failed?
- Does anyone see a pattern emerging?
- Key question.
- What might be a new solution?

These are the questions you might pose to the group. Behind each one you would have half a page of notes, examples, quotes. Then, if your bare question provoked nothing but coughs, you could talk a little, reminding them of what you meant, encouraging them to say something.

When you launch a discussion, you cannot let it ramble. The audience expects you to have a point. You can take almost any comment and turn it back to your purpose, if you have anticipated the reactions you're likely to get from each question, and thought out paths leading back to your argument.

You have to let them have their say, without giving up your own position. And you need to think out your own arguments beforehand. (It's too late to think things over when you're standing up there in front of the group.)

In fact, the better you know your own ideas, the easier it will be for you to encourage people who disagree with you, or who wander off the topic. You know where you stand, and after waiting a while, you can make your disagreement clear, without bullying them or bulling around. You can then bring up your initial question again, looking for further answers.

In planning out these questions, make sure that you can really stand the answers. Some subjects elicit violent reactions. If you think that might happen, consider whether or not you can show that you've had similar feelings. What will you do if you're personally attacked? How are you going to admit error, or defend your company and your boss?

Don't count on getting real agreement easily. You can force everyone to nod together, but that won't mean they've thought the question through and reached a heart-felt pact. You can't build on it. Only by opening yourself up to a real exchange of views will you lay down the basis for eventual consensus.

In many circumstances, you'll be stirring up a conflict between two sides. If you want both sides to talk, you'll have to be genially uncommitted, at least until the yelling dies down. So think very carefully about how to phrase your questions and responses, eliminating any phrases that suggest you agree with one side or the other.

A discussion takes more preparation than a straight lecture. And the audience isn't aware of this preparation, since the talk looks impromptu. But if you don't think through all the possible routes the conversation may take, you may end up with a fight, a stalled and sullen group, or a confusing mess.

Present, Don't Lecture

In college courses, professors lecture. In training, you present. The difference: you use more visuals, you make more effort to help people remember your main points, you adapt what you say to the changing moods of the audience. Keep training presentations short. Interrupt them with demonstrations, activities, slides, videotapes, graphics. Never go longer than forty-five minutes at one time.

The key to memorable presentations is a clear structure, one that's easy to sum up in three to five short phrases. Take each major idea, and put it into a verb phrase. Not "Responsibility for Purchase Decision," but "Deciding on a Purchase."

Those phrases should go on your flipchart and on your handouts. You'll use them to introduce the lesson, then to head each phase within the lesson. That way people understand that there is a pattern to look for, and they can make mental checkmarks as you reach each phase. Then you can repeat the phrases, as an aide-mémoire at the end.

Having a simple, easily stated outline helps you in another way. When you have a firm design like that, you can expand or contract sections without confusing people. Thus, if you notice that people already know a lot of what you were about to say, you can scrap a few pages of explanation and go onto the next point.

Listening is what lets you adapt your notes to the mood of the audience. But you need to be prepared to run longer, if they seem confused, or if they want more explanations. So each phrase should head a page or two of notes.

Those notes should include more examples than you will really want to use. In addition to examples, collect some quotations. They add another voice to your own.

And while you're thinking about illustrations, look for pictures. You might draw some cartoons on the flipcharts, with each phrase. Or you could cut out photographs to project as slides. These amuse the wandering eye, and reinforce your message.

Monitor Those Activities

To get people out of their seats and moving around, plan some activity. Rehearsing the procedures you're training helps everyone learn them. But a poorly planned activity—or one you don't oversee with care—will degenerate into a hubbub.

First explain why they should bother. Set the activity in a context. You can point out the benefits, the relevance to your main topic. Inspire the audience to take part—not just go along.

And you'll need to figure out exactly what you want people to do. If you don't think the instructions through, your planned activity will quickly come apart. Write the rules down on a piece of paper for each person to hold. Put them on a flipchart. Go over them with the group, then walk around the group as they begin and make sure that they are really following these rules. (They won't be.)

That's monitoring. Plan what you're going to have to expect. Figure out the most common ways people can foul up. If you can, test out your instructions beforehand on several other people, to see how they misinterpret them. Revise accordingly.

The best planned activities require people to work with each other, carrying out some physical task. So you might imagine some scenario, a little drama. That will help people get into the activity with some gusto.

But remember: an activity only helps when each person understands the goal and the procedures.

Test and Test Again

At the end of a training session, test. See if the participants can meet the objectives you set up at the start.

The point of this test is not to make a lot of people flunk. In fact, if you've done your homework well, everyone will pass. In school, tests helped to sort us out into A, B, C, D, and worse. But here there are only two grades: pass or fail. That's because we want visual evidence that people can perform as planned—or not.

There are no points for almost making it. And if more than one or two people fail to meet the criteria you set up at the start, you can figure that there was something wrong with your training.

You're not creating an essay test. Each question measures

the participant against the objective standards you announced at the start. So be sure you don't change the rules on people at the end, and give a question that asks for history or art appreciation, instead of actual performance. See what they can do.

Was the objective achieved? If so, your training succeeded. If not, you need to revise it. Don't be discouraged by that. Most professionals revise a training program five or six times before it begins to succeed with 60 or 70 percent of the participants.

Summary

Since the purpose of training is to help people pass—that is, to change their behavior in a way that meets measurable criteria—you give away the answers before the test. At least, you try.

A summary helps. It might be very similar to the outline you provided at the start of training. Same points. Same phrases. Same order. Just repeating it all again—only this time, with new meaning.

To sum up training techniques:

- Analyze before you write.
- Define your objectives.
- Get it in order.
- Use a variety of training techniques.
- Warm-ups.
- Lead a discussion.
- Present, don't lecture.
- Monitor those activities.
- Test, and test again.

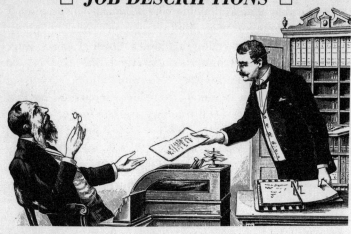

S
o your boss wants you to describe what you do. Before you start, ask why.

The company may use that job description for any of these purposes:

- to help your boss evaluate your work;
- to justify your promotion;
- to develop new career paths for you;
- to fit you into some new organization chart—or to lop you off as superfluous;
- to distinguish your job from ones at a higher or lower pay level, and to group your job with others in a similar category;
- to tell the training and personnel people what actually goes on at your level;
- to write a help-wanted ad for someone to replace you or to work in a similar job, as well as to give the personnel department some way of rejecting candidates as "unqualified";

- to show a new employee what kind of work is involved in this job;
- to help the company defend itself against suits brought under the Equal Pay Act and Equal Employment Opportunity Act;
- to wrangle with unions over the qualifications needed for your job.

The more you know about the reasons behind the request for a job description, the easier it'll be to write. If the company plans to use it in fighting off a union or a disgruntled job applicant, your description's going to be tested by lawyers, so you'd better not exaggerate what you have to know and what you have to do in your job.

The first temptation, though, is to throw down a few abstract phrases, add some jargon, and send it off. Resist it. You're under scrutiny, even if the boss says this is just a routine. And if you settle for a bunch of phrases that sound like a want ad or the work of a Human Resources expert, you'll miss an opportunity.

In general, what you write can advertise what a great job you're doing, and how hard it will be to replace you. In the process of creating your job description, you can also begin to see how much you already do—and that will give you some new ideas for your résumé.

Your company probably has its own form for job descriptions, drawn up by someone who never thought much about your job. You'll see a bunch of topics, arranged under a series of categories, with abstract titles. The most common categories follow, with some hints on what to say about each.

What You Do

Don't generalize too fast. Take a look at your schedule and write down what you've been working on in the last quarter.

- What are your biggest successes?
- What does your boss care about?
- What problems have you had to face?
- What little jobs do you take care of?
- What odd jobs—infrequent or emergency—have you sometimes done?
- What do you ask your staff to do? What do you do for them? How do you monitor their work?
- What reports do you have to turn in?
- Have you had to train anyone?
- Do you hire or fire? Handle promotions?

When you have twenty or so of these activities down on paper, sort them out into half a dozen larger tasks. For instance, you might start out with some notes like this:

Talked to George about video in next season's marketing

Wrote script

Lined up support for marketing plan

Made up marketing plan

Got approvals (Joe, Sue, Ivan, Edwina)

Supervised Bill

Trained our two new employees, Al and Evie

Set up budget

Got staff to write own quarterly plans (objectives, deadlines)

Then you could bunch those together in general terms:

Create marketing plans for our division

Supervise staff (agree on quarterly objectives, deadlines, monitor performance, give feedback)

Train new employees

Establish and monitor budget

Develop ways of communicating marketing plans
(video, slide, brochure)

Some of your notes may end up in other sections, and some
may get squashed together into one phrase. You'll find other
ideas as you explore the other categories, so leave room. Add
figures, if you've overlooked them. For instance, you could rewrite two of these activities this way:

Supervise staff of four (agree on quarterly objectives,
deadlines, monitor performance, give feedback)
Establish and monitor $240,000 departmental budget

Your Main Objectives

Even broader than the first section are general policies you
have to carry out. Often these "objectives" correspond to a
business plan you've received, or agreed upon. In this section,
then, you show how what you do helps the company meet its
long-term goals.

If you're puzzled about your objectives, ask yourself:

- How does my work further our business plan?
- What would the boss say that I produce for the company?
- What do I provide to other departments, or to my superiors?
- What do I receive from other departments, and pass
along with improvements?

You're looking at your job from the boss's point of view.
What good are you? How are you carrying out the major mis-
sion of your department?

What You Are Responsible For

Similar to the first category, this one defines what you're
held responsible for in a formal way—for instance, regular re-

ports, production quotas, budget preparation. (You may find you're repeating yourself.)

Leave out the informal responsibilities—tasks you do occasionally, on your own, without specific orders from your boss. Leave out emergency troubleshooting, unless that tends to get routine. Leave out reporting relationships you have with other departments.

Who You Work With

Not the names, the titles. Who do you report to directly? Who do you inform of your decisions, even if they aren't your superiors? Who do you have to consult before reaching a decision? Who has to approve what types of decision before you carry them out?

And who do you have to cooperate with? Think of all the people you deal with in an average week. Don't exclude people just because they're not on some approval form. Informal contacts count. Also, who do you help, and how?

The easiest names to recall—and the most important—are the people you train, or supervise. You can sort these relationships out this way:

- Report directly to _____
- Consult with _____ before decisions involving _____
- Secure approval from _____ on decisions involving _____
- Notify _____ about all decisions involving _____
- Provide _____ with _____
- Cooperate with _____ on _____
- Train _____ in _____
- Supervise _____
- Coordinate the work of _____ and _____
- Interview _____ about _____

- Hire _____
- Evaluate _____
- Make promotion recommendations for _____
- Resolve problems between _____ and _____

Where You Can Go from Here
(Possible Career Paths)

If you have strict promotion paths at your company, mention the next positions in here. If not, put in the ones that correspond to what you aim to do, and what you've told your boss about your ambitions.

Standards by Which You Are Judged

You're often judged on your personality. Some bosses rate you on a list of character traits you're supposed to display: attitude, cooperativeness, creativity, dependability, efficiency, energy, flexibility, independence, and leadership.

Avoid suggesting that you be judged by personality traits. Your boss's definition of "attitude" may not be yours. And although it's wonderful to have all these traits, it's hard to know how to get them, or demonstrate them, so if the boss says you're lacking in creativity, you may be at a loss to know how to improve.

If possible, put down numbers by which you can be measured. At least include measurable results. For instance:

Meet monthly production quota.
Come in under quarterly budget.
Keep mean time between failure above 1000 hours.

The higher you go, the harder it is to measure your job quantitatively. Think in terms of minimums, then:

Maintain market share for our four leading products.
Keep return on investment above 15%.
Introduce three new products each year.

Don't make these standards too high; you might actually be judged by them.

Tools You Use

Your pen. Your computer. Your car. Any equipment at all. Give yourself the benefit of the doubt. If you can run a slide projector after someone's showed you where the buttons are, put that down. And don't forget the copying machine.

What Safety Precautions You Have to Take

You probably won't have to answer this. But if safety's an activity—something you actually do—then write it up in the same way you did the other tasks you perform. For instance:

Secure all bolts before operation.
Lock down hatch covers.
Put on goggles, gloves, steel-tip boots, hard hat.
Check that plugs are in securely.

Education, Training, and Experience Required

This is want-ad stuff. Just put in what's really required. For instance, can you prove that a college degree is required? Are there some people doing your job without one?

Since this material defines minimum standards for hiring, you must be accurate. Does someone really need five years experience to do this job? Exactly why? Can you spell out the particular skills needed? Which certificate or license do you have to have?

Think as if you were working in the personnel department,

trying to distinguish between acceptable and unacceptable candidates for your job. Or imagine you were applying. (Don't make the standards so tough you wouldn't get hired.)

If you got into the job without training, but now think anyone else must have some, put that here, but be very specific about what kind, and how much. You're venturing onto dangerous ground. If you think your job description will be read by lawyers, develop some explanation—perhaps the nature of the job has changed since you came.

If some training, experience, or skill is helpful, but not absolutely required, put that in the next section. Again, if the company gets into a battle over your job description, lawyers are going to ask you questions like, "But is this really required? Or is it just a frivolous 'standard' designed to keep our clients out?"

Education, Training, and Experience Not Required, but Helpful

Feel free to improvise in this section. Make the list as long as you like—languages, courses, grade levels, machines, skills. Since these aren't required, you can make the job seem more important than it is by decorating it with education.

Now That You're Through . . .

You may feel that all this work means nothing—and in some cases, that's true. But think of it this way: writing your job description gives you a lot of material for your résumé.

W ouldn't it be great if you had a machine that could evaluate every employee, so you wouldn't have to write up evaluations? Some personnel departments think they have a scientific system for rating and motivating employees, but even the best of these depends on your good judgment and common sense.

Of course, reviewing an employee who's doing well isn't too

hard. You just have to think of enough to say to fill up the
form. But you face more difficulties with employees who are
plodding along without inspiration, or causing problems. What
do you say about people who:

- don't think straight and can't remember rules;
- just do what they've always done, even though conditions have changed;
- take a hostile attitude to anyone who walks into the
  office;
- argue about small matters and ignore large issues;
- bring meetings to their knees with quibbling or ob-
  structionism; or
- drive fellow workers crazy with pickiness, pettifog-
  gery, laziness, finger-pointing, or lying.

You can't force these people to grow up. You can't assign
them to spend three hours a week talking with a therapist.
And, alas, you can't dispatch them with a one-way ticket to
your competition's front door.

So you write on their evaluation, "Should improve attitude." But that's so subjective that the employee can legiti-
mately claim, "I improved my attitude! But you still don't
like me."

What you need is a plan.

Plan Before You Evaluate

In a meeting with the employee, set up a number of measurable objectives you expect the employee to meet by the end of
the review period. Ask the employee to come up with some,
too. Typical goals:

- key projects you want the employee to finish in this
  time period;
- regular workload you want turned around in a week;

- new assignments you want added to the regular work-load, with a specific turnaround time for each one;
- training the employee wants for future career moves (specific courses); and
- tests, qualifying boards, certificate programs the employee wants to pass for career advancement.

Don't set too many objectives; you're going to hold the employee accountable for achieving them, so don't impose an impossible burden. But the objectives you do set must be measurable.

I say measurable, because you want to have a guideline you can both agree on, beforehand and afterward. For instance, the product got out the door, or it didn't. The report was written, or wasn't. Sales went up by 5 percent, or they didn't.

Too many objectives sound commendable, but are essentially unmeasurable. The employee must agree that he or she should become more assertive in dealing with deadbeat customers; at the end of the review period, you could think this person was just as plaintive as before, whereas the employee thinks he or she was loud and aggressive. It's subjective, so you can both argue about it for hours and come to no conclusion.

So set up objectives that can be put in terms of numbers, delivery dates, product—not attitude. Be sure that these reflect what you really want from the employee. (You can't change your mind next week.) And listen to the employee's view of what's possible. Both of you must agree these are reasonable.

Ask for a Self-Evaluation

When the review period comes to a close, ask your employees to write their own reviews. Ask them to write up:

- which objectives they met;
- which they surpassed;

- which they failed to accomplish—and why;
- which ones you told them to forget because your priorities changed; and
- what objectives they think they should set for the next review period.

Ask for a page or two, at most. You'll learn a lot from this, especially what the employees consider important, irritating, or impossible.

These self-evaluations should also help you to keep your mind on achievement, not just gut reactions. Then you can start writing your review.

Weigh Accomplishments First

Start by discussing each achievement. No matter how slender, each accomplishment deserves praise. Your employees will usually get to read what you write—sooner or later. And you can organize your discussions with them by proceeding from praise to questions, postponing threats and demands to the end.

Force yourself to distribute praise for each objective met or surpassed. A lot of us find it hard to tell others they've done well. If you clam up like this, you can find inspiration by considering questions like these about each objective:

- Has the employee outperformed the average? In what areas?
- What comments did other people make about this accomplishment?
- How much money did this activity bring in or save?
- In what ways did the employee surpass the objective?
- What personal ideas, innovations, methods did the employee contribute to this activity?
- In what ways did your department and company benefit from this accomplishment?

When you turn to the objectives the employees *didn't* achieve, pay particular attention to their explanation.

- Does it make sense?
- Is it consistent with earlier explanations?
- In what ways is their failure your fault?
- Did department or company objectives change, making it pointless for the employee to proceed?
- Now that you think about it, do you still believe the objective was reasonable and achievable?
- Having made all the allowances you can, do you still think the employee fouled up?

Put off blaming an employee until you have no other way to explain the failure. Even then, resist the temptation to let loose with the expletives. You risk libel suits, and you don't improve anyone's performance that way.

Keep your comments quantitative, where possible. For instance:

- How much did this failure cost your department or company?
- How long will other projects be delayed because of this employee?
- What comments have been received from customers, other departments, other staff members?
- How has this failure affected the productivity rating of your group?

Avoid putting threats in writing. If you really are going to put them on notice, check with your boss and your conscience: are you willing to follow through on your threatened punishment? If not, you are going to lose authority when your bluff is called.

In general, postpone any blame until you actually meet with the employees and discuss these missed objectives. You may find out more than their self-review indicated. You may also discover ways to change procedures, so people find it easier to work together. After all, your main effort should be to improve performance, not issue damaging critiques.

Discuss What to Do Next, Not Who Did What Wrong

Use your discussion with the employees to figure out better procedures, better plans, better staff arrangements. Look for solutions, not scapegoats. And as you talk, take notes for your final review.

By focusing on the future—the objectives for the employees next time period, including any changes to help them meet these goals—you can avoid fruitless debates about who's to blame.

At the end of your discussion, show your notes to the employee to make sure you both agree on what should be done next. Use them in making up a rough draft of your final review. During this process, you'll probably find you have to add some new objectives to your own plan.

Save Qualitative Comments for Promotion Recommendations

When you've finished the review and have made up your mind to promote or give a raise, you can indulge in some of the subjective evaluation that we all enjoy. And that's where it belongs: in a letter of congratulations, rather than in a serious review.

Here are some of the adjectives you might want to pull out at such a time: *independent, flexible, thorough, innovative, diplomatic, cooperative, articulate.*

But in your actual review, resist the temptation to use words like these or their opposites. If you call people "undiplomatic," how can they improve? What concrete steps can they take to measure up to your standard?

So keep the review separate from such commentary. Otherwise, employees will start arguing over the subjective issues, saying, "But I'm just as cooperative as Sue, and she got a raise, so I should get one."

In Conclusion

To keep your discussion and review focused on measurable actions an employee can take, you'll need to do more than write. The talking, the collaborating helps you formulate plans that both of you understand. This way, writing is almost an afterthought, a report on what you've already worked out.

So when review time rolls around, keep these guidelines in mind:

- Plan before you evaluate.
- Ask for a self-evaluation.
- Weigh accomplishments first.
- Discuss what to do next, not who did what wrong.
- Save qualitative comments for promotion recommendations.

☐ *RÉSUMÉS* ☐

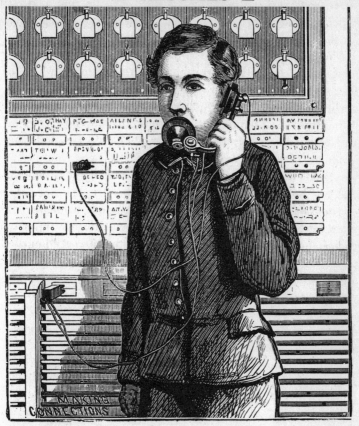

When you're looking for a job, call all your friends, your family, former co-workers, anyone who's doing the kind of job you want. Tell them what you're after. Your best leads come from tips—not ads. And studies show that the more places you look, the faster you'll find a new job.

A résumé alone won't get you a job. But once you've found an opening, a well-written résumé could help you get an interview. And after the interview, it will speak for you as your papers circulate through the new company, making it easier for them to offer you the job you want.

Most résumés get looked at for less than ten seconds. And most get rejected. Here are some of the ways to get rejected fast: saying you want a job that's different from the one that's open; filling the page up so no one can find out what you do without spending ten minutes of painful reading; forgetting to highlight skills (most people seem to highlight dates—and the heading "résumé"); and leaving out information that shows you can do the job you are applying for—even if you never had that title before.

Some other ways to get tossed in the trash: using an old typewriter that kicks every *t* above the line; making gray copies of dim originals, then writing in corrections with a ballpoint pen; printing your résumé on some unusual paper; leaving off your address and phone number, so no one can reach you (it happens!), and playing hard to get; not giving much detail about what you've accomplished or produced; leaving out dollars, awards, and statistics; and emphasizing routine chores rather than successes, and sounding slightly bored.

Given this kind of competition, a well-designed résumé can help you get noticed and invited in for an interview. When written with a particular job opening in mind, your résumé can show the employer:

- You know what skills this job requires—and you have them.
- You've already accomplished a lot, had some big successes.
- You understand the kind of information an employer wants to know, so you'll probably get along well on the job. You mention dollars, production figures, number of people you supervised. You use a few key terms, without loading the page with jargon.

- You can prepare a document that's pleasant to look at and interesting to read.
- You make things easy for prospective employers—by including both your home and work phone numbers, for instance.

The Top of the Page

Some people figure the employer will not recognize that this sheet of paper is a résumé, so they roll down an inch or two, center the word "RÉSUMÉ" up there, then drop down another inch or so before mentioning their name and address. This wastes paper. And it focuses attention—remember, you can only count on ten seconds' worth, at first—on something that says nothing about you.

A résumé is supposed to sell *you*. So put your name up on top. Isolate your name from your address. Put your address over on the left, a few lines below. Put your phone numbers over on the right, where they're easier to find when someone decides to call you. Like this:

JEROME BOSCH

1321 Callaway Way   Home: (415) 525–6565
Berkeley, CA 94707   Work: (415) 525–8776

The next item should be the job you're after. Stating your job objective reassures the employer. It shows you really want this job, and not something else. It shows you've made at least that much commitment to the job.

Some applicants put half a dozen jobs here, to show they're willing to do anything. But employers figure that if you can't make up your mind what you want to do, why should they risk hiring you, only to find you change jobs three months later? So include only one job objective per résumé.

Make sure you use the title the employer mentioned in the ad or notice. You may call the job "auditing," but the employer wants an "internal auditor," so say that's what you want to be. If you aren't sure, call the employer and ask what the title is. Most people will use the wrong name for the job, and some will get rejected just because of that.

So the top of your résumé might look like this:

JEROME BOSCH

1321 Callaway Way	Home: (415) 525–6565
Berkeley, CA 94707	Work: (415) 525–8776

JOB OBJECTIVE: Internal Auditor

A word about format. There is no perfect layout for a résumé, although there are many that look cramped, stuffy, or difficult. If you like moving items around, fine. Just keep some general principles in mind.

Emphasize what you want the employer to notice in the first glance: your name, the job you're after, and your main qualifications. Downplay the less important—or embarrassing—information.

Among the things you should deemphasize are:

- Exact dates, company names, job titles from your past. You should *include* these, but they're not the *crucial* data. Once the employer sees you have certain skills, he'll want to see what your jobs were. But unless you've had prestigious jobs at top companies, the title and company name won't sell you. Your abilities do.
- Jobs that aren't relevant to this one. The employer may decide that's all you can do.
- Schooling, if you've been out of school for a few years. Mention your education last, and consider omitting the years. So what if you dropped out of school for a while?
- Hobbies (not necessary).
- Names of references. Say they're available on re-

quest, so the people don't get pestered with calls, and so their names don't clutter up your résumé.

Make it easy for employers to find things when they actually settle down to read your résumé. For instance, separating the phone numbers from the address helps the eye find a phone number a little faster than if you clump all that information together.

The Guts: Your Skills

The guts of your résumé are your skills. That's what will convince someone to call you in for an interview. So the middle of your résumé should focus on what you can do for the employer. I recommend two sections: "Skills" and "Job History."

Skills go first. You could call this section "Abilities," "Interests," or "Work Experience." Within it, highlight three or four major skills, such as "Organizing," "Forecasting," or "Budgeting." Those skills, of course, should correspond to the main tasks you'll be called on to perform in your new job.

And on the right, separated out into distinct and readable chunks, you can put the details that prove you have exercised these skills already. For instance, you might write:

ORGANIZING:

- Set up German manufacturing division in record time. $18 million capitalization; two factories built and brought up to speed in two years. Division became profitable in third year.
- Reorganized headquarters staff of 130. Established new reporting relationships, reduced number of vice presidents, increased flow of information within top management.

- Launched hospital fund-raising drive, involving more than 150 people over three years. Secured $15 million private financing and $10 million in government grants.

That's what catches an employer's eye. Later you can mention what dates you worked in what job slot at which company. Too many résumés look as if the key fact about the applicant is a series of dates. Those dates hang out in the lefthand margin, facing a black haze of text. So most people tend to read the dates, and skip the background.

The second section, then, backs up your first one. It provides more traditional résumé data:

- The dates you worked at each job;
- The title of your position;
- The name and address of the company;
- For each school after grammar school, the date of graduation, name of school, and address.

Since you've outlined your skills above, you don't need to add much detail about each job, as you would in an old-fashioned résumé. And you'll only need to include information about your education if you're a recent grad or switching careers.

Essentially, you are figuring out what the employer most wants to know, and putting that on the upper half of the page, where he'll glance at it first. You don't want him to spend fifteen minutes figuring out whether you will be right. You are showing you know the job—and have already acquired the necessary skills.

Figuring Out Your Skills

At first, you may find it hard to think what skills you already have. So go through the following list, checking off any action you've performed, whether or not it was for pay, whether or not it was on a job like the one you're after. Have you ever done this? Could you do it again? If so, check it.

And then, on the right, add details. For instance, if you check "REPAIRED," put down what you fixed.

After a while, you'll notice some patterns emerging. Ask yourself whether you can bunch these skills together in categories. Don't force this; just keep an eye out for it. You'll probably find half a dozen categories, some leading right to the job you want, some irrelevant. That's fine.

Don't censor. If you've done something, take credit for it. Don't be high-minded and say that because you didn't do it brilliantly, you can't do it. If you can do it, check it. If you're brilliant at it, fine: just add the details, so the boss will know.

DID THIS:

ACQUIRED	COORDINATED	FORECAST
ADMINISTERED	CREATED	GAINED SUPPORT
ADVISED	DEALT WITH	FOR
ANALYZED	PUBLIC	GAVE DIRECTIONS
ANTICIPATED	DEMONSTRATED	GREW
ARRANGED	DESCRIBED	GUIDED
ASSEMBLED	DESIGNED	HAD RESPONSIBIL-
ASSESSED	DETERMINED	ITY FOR
ATTENDED	GOALS, AND	HANDLED COM-
AUDITED	POLICIES	PLAINTS
BUDGETED	DEVELOPED	HELPED
BUILT	DISCIPLINED	HIRED
CALCULATED	DISTRIBUTED	IDENTIFIED
CHANGED	EARNED	IMPLEMENTED
CLASSIFIED	EDITED	IMPROVED
COMMUNICATED	ESTABLISHED	INCREASED
CONTRIBUTED TO	PRIORITIES	INITIATED
CONTROLLED	ESTIMATED	INSPECTED
COOPERATED	EVALUATED	INSTALLED
WITH	EXPLORED	INTERVIEWED

INVENTED	PLANNED	SECURED GRANTS
INVENTORIED	PREPARED AGENDAS	SET A RECORD
ISSUED	PRESENTED TO	SET UP SYSTEMS
JUDGED	THE PUBLIC	SOLD
KEPT THE BOOKS	PREVENTED	SOLVED
LECTURED	PRODUCED	STANDARDIZED
MADE	PROGRAMMED	SUBMITTED
MANAGED	PROMOTED	SUPERVISED
MARKETED	PROVIDED	TALKED WITH
MOTIVATED	RECORDED	TAUGHT
NEGOTIATED	RECRUITED	TESTED
OPERATED	RECYCLED	TRAINED
ORGANIZED	REPAIRED	USED LANGUAGES
PARTICIPATED IN	REPORTED	VERIFIED
PERFORMED	RESEARCHED	WON (PROMOTION,
PERSUADED	SAVED	PRIZE)
PILOTED	SCHEDULED	WROTE

Now that you see how easy it is to view your work in terms of skills, go back through your major jobs to see how you would describe each. Remember to start with an active verb in the past tense. "Supervised" sounds more energetic than "Was responsible for." Active verbs are often clearer, too.

And finally, figure out your skills: think what skills are needed on the job you're applying for. Then go back through all your work experience, your hobbies, your schooldays, and see how many pertinent examples you can come up with—times when you did something like that. Don't worry about the fact that you did it when your job title was very different. You're interested in the skill, not the personnel file.

The point is to turn up other skills you may have overlooked. Also, to prepare you to talk about those jobs in terms an employer can understand—not your title, or rank, but what you actually did.

When you feel you've milked your work history dry, arrange

these skills in groups. For instance, if you checked "LECTURED," "TALKED," and "WROTE," you could list those with their details under a heading like "COMMUNICATION SKILLS."

COMMUNICATION SKILLS:

- LECTURED to 600 participants in industry seminars at trade shows.
- TALKED with more than fifty community groups, as part of headquarters' goodwill effort.
- WROTE ten articles for trade publications, discussing our products. Also, four brochures explaining our division to new employees.

Now you may have lectured while at one company, talked while at another, and written at a third. But from a new employer's point of view, the important fact is that you can communicate. So break that skill out.

Summarizing Your Skills

To apply these descriptions to your résumé, you'll have to analyze the job you're applying for. What types of skills are needed there? And which will be the most important?

If you're reading an ad, that may give some clue. For instance, if the ad asks for someone innovative, you'll want to see what you've got under "CREATED" and "INVENTED," say, and group those under a heading such as "INNOVATIONS." Adapt your vocabulary to the ad. Shuffle your skills to fit the job.

Three or four groups of skills, with two or three items in each, are enough. Don't exhaust your readers. They want an outline, not an encyclopedia.

Put the skills that are most relevant to the job first. For instance, if the person who told you about the job mentioned that the employer wants "a real manager, not just a time server," you could start off like this:

SUPERVISORY EXPERIENCE (FOUR YEARS):

- ESTABLISHED policy and set standards for group of fifteen engineers.
- BROUGHT in 85 percent of projects on time and under budget.
- ADMINISTERED $500,000 budget. Prepared monthly and quarterly financial reports for company and government.

Notice that this person has put "experience" instead of "skills." That's fine. In fact, you could call this section "Work Experience" and the next one "Work History."

Note that in parentheses this writer has put the number of years he's had supervisory experience. This way he can combine supervision done in three different jobs at two different companies, to show he has solid credentials. If you've acquired a skill at several companies, you may want to add up the total number of years and put that here, to indicate the skill has been acquired over a long time. This also helps draw attention away from possibly embarrassing gaps in your work history.

Here is how one woman summed up her skills:

AUDITING EXPERIENCE (THREE YEARS):

- PERFORMED complete compliance audit on pension plan. Validated quarterly financial statements of three Fortune 1000 companies.
- PLANNED follow-ups on twelve earlier compliance audits.
- SET UP guidelines for financial audits in $100-million-a-year corporation.

SUPERVISORY EXPERIENCE (TWO YEARS):

- ADMINISTERED preaudit contacts, fieldwork of five internal auditors.
- ESTABLISHED internal audit plan. Worked with senior vice presidents to change priorities and schedules.
- HIRED and trained internal auditors.

COMMUNICATION EXPERIENCE (FIVE YEARS):

- WROTE two dozen audit reports with management summaries.
- LECTURED on innovations in audit practice before national convention.
- PREPARED individual audit programs for internal auditors to follow.

Putting in the Dates

If you just list your skills and nothing else, employers will wonder if you ever had a job. That's why you need to add a section detailing where you worked and when.

Start with the most recent job and go back in time. Put the dates out in the left margin; then your job title; then the company name and address.

1981–1983	Municipal Bond Salesman, Rawson McKinna, 1530 Alamo Avenue, Houston, Texas
1978–1981	Investment Counselor, First City Bank of Central Texas, 18 West Sheridan Street, Houston, Texas

If you've got an unbroken work history, one long-term job after another since school, this presentation will make you look good.

But it can get embarrassing if you went without a job for three years, or had five jobs in six months, or never did the job you're applying for. That's another reason why we drop this material to the bottom of the page, so you won't get rejected right off.

If you've been out of a job for a period of more than a year put your job titles in the left margin, and place the dates in parentheses at the end of the company address.

Municipal Bond Salesman   Rawson McKinna, 1530 Alamo Avenue, Houston, Texas (1981–1982)

Investment Counselor   First City Bank of Central Texas, 18 West Sheridan Street, Houston, Texas (1978–1979)

That draws attention away from those two years of unemployment in 1980 and 1983. You're not lying, but you are covering up.

If you've had a lot of short-term jobs, pick one or two and put the year, not the months. I've seen résumés that had left margins like this:

January–February, 1982

March, 1982

April–May, 1982

July, 1982

September–October, 1982

December, 1982

That person may have been steadily working at a series of temporary jobs, but it looks like he got fired or just quit——a lot. Better to limit yourself to two or three job titles, and at the very end of each company's address, just put the year you worked there.

Where possible, pick a job title that sounds like the one you're applying for. Include volunteer jobs, without calling them volunteer. What you did in the military counts—just give it a civilian name, if possible.

Put your education last. Follow the same format you've used for your work history. In other words, if you put dates first there, put them first here. Just put a date of graduation.

1977   B.A. in Business and Accounting, University of Washington.

1979   M.B.A. with specialization in International Finance, University of Washington.

If you've taken some university, military, or conference seminars in the area you want to work in, mention those, and give a few details. If you've only been out of school for a year or so, say more about the courses you took. Feel free to describe those courses in a way that your employer will recognize—even if the college registrar might not. Leave out the courses that aren't relevant to the job you're after.

1980   Credit Policies—three-month course by Army Supply Command.

1981   Advanced Purchasing—two-month course by Army Supply Command. Inventory control, control of purchase orders, online access to Army purchasing data base.

Leave out the usual "personal data" unless you really care. Hobbies, special interests, other skills—these are fine, but only if they're real. If you put down "soccer, jogging, and history," you may be asked a lot of intense questions by a boss who just happens to know the history of soccer. So don't mention something unless you are an aficionado.

Revising Your Résumé—Perpetually

Several university studies suggest that most unemployed people spend less than five hours a week looking for work. I'd recommend you spend forty. That's eight times what other people do. You increase your odds that way.

You can figure to spend half that week getting in touch with employers, and the other half of the week writing, and rewriting, your résumé. You probably thought you could write it once, print it, and that would be it. Not true.

You may have to create several slightly different résumés for the different types of job you're applying for. In fact, I'd recommend you type up a new one for every opening. Customizing your whole résumé helps you show the employers that you're exactly the person they're looking for. You use their terms on your résumé. You arrange your experience to match their ad. You show familiarity with their products—and it's right there on the résumé.

Obviously you don't have to rewrite the whole résumé. Usually your revisions will home in on what you say about your skills—rearranging entries, renaming categories, moving one example up to first place, leaving another out. You are editing to appeal to whatever you know about the employers.

- What skills do they think most important?
- What jobs apply most directly?
- Which courses?
- What terms, titles, jargon does this company use?

Once you see your résumé as an artifact—something left over from your continuous rewriting—you won't worry so much about changing it every day. In fact, you'll polish a new skill: résumé-writing.

Cover Letters

Yes, always send one. But don't waste it telling the employer that you are sending him a résumé. That's obvious.

Instead, say you want to work for them. "I want to work for you as a ..." Then jump to the key points of your résumé—the ones that will most interest this particular employer. Introduce these with a sentence like "Here are some of the highlights of my experience."

Pick out three significant successes from your résumé. Give each a sentence or two. Separate them with white space. Then sign off.

A cover letter should tease the reader into turning the page and looking at your attached résumé. Most writers assume the reader has fifteen uninterrupted minutes to read through whole paragraphs that only say, basically, "I'm applying for that job in the paper. Here's my résumé." That doesn't intrigue anyone—it's just exhausting.

By singling out your biggest achievements, you advertise your best points. You give the employer a reason to read on.

Summing Up

- Start with your name—not the word "résumé."
- Make it easy to spot your phone number and address.
- State your job objective:
      Just one
      Use the same title the boss does.
- Stress your skills:
      Isolate each type
      Highlight each achievement.

- Downplay the dates:
  Mention job title, company, address, and dates you
  worked there—but put this information at the bot-
  tom of the page.
- Revise your résumé perpetually.
- Yes, add a cover letter:
  Say you want the job
  Single out your major achievements
  Don't ramble on.

▪ *Help Others Write Well* ▪

□ *HELP OTHERS WRITE WELL* □

Persuading your staff to write clearly takes so much effort you may feel you're gouging coal out of a mine. Who's really cooperating? Who's loafing? And how can you get everyone digging together?

First, realize this takes months. You're changing habits of many years' standing. Few employees will believe you mean what you say; most will resist.

So start by calling a special meeting. Explain why you think that clear writing is part of the job—not just some incidental extra. Writing's part of what your team produces; it establishes your reputation with people who rarely get to meet you—inside or outside of the corporation. Important decisions depend on it, since bosses can only act on what they understand.

Then make sure you're turning out understandable prose yourself. Ask co-workers, secretaries, recipients if they could follow what you were saying. Probe. Was there some part of your letter that seemed murky? Did they feel you left something out? Ran on too long about something else? Did you put things in order, as far as they were concerned?

When you show that you're willing to listen, you also indicate how you want people to react to your own suggestions. So take advice. Rewrite and show them how you followed their ideas.

Set up some classes, too—and take them along with your people. Turn to experts in the company, or find outside consultants, teachers, writers. You can get training on memos and letters, proposals, technical documentation about scientific, mechanical, or computer processes, and specific problems of style.

Don't let up. When you see a particularly awful piece of writing from outside the company, circle it and send around a copy with your comments. Don't rip apart one of your own staff's letters, though. When someone on your team writes a snappy memo, send congratulations, and make sure that everybody else hears about it.

Whenever you notice that a lot of people are stumbling into the same mistake, make that the subject of a memo. Encourage the staff to send around similar memos. And if someone comes up with an idea that could help everyone write better, push for it, even if it's going to cost money.

Edit important documents before they go out. But don't become a bottleneck. Do it fast. One way to speed up your editing is to distinguish between versions.

1. ROUGH DRAFT. Concentrate on key points of organization, general style. Don't bother with typos or little turns of phrase.
2. FINAL DRAFT. Do a thorough combing. (This takes the longest.)
3. REVISED FINAL DRAFT. Clean up small points; do not ask for any major reworking unless the situation has changed. (This assumes you spotted all the reorganization needed, and the writer took your advice.)

4. APPROVED FINAL DRAFT. This is the one going to a printer. Enter only typesetting codes or formats.

Working on the first three versions of a document, you'll be reading as you would to revise your own work. Imagine yourself as one of the recipients, and look at it from their point of view. You might ask these questions:

1. On the rough draft:
   Is the subject clear?
   Is the point visible?
   Does the organization support the point?
   Is any major section missing?
   Should something be cut?
   Which spots seem confusing or weak?
   Which transitions seem jerky or forced?
   Is the vocabulary appropriate for the audience?
   Is the style plain enough?
2. On the final draft:
   Have all the questions raised before been acted on?
   Is the text accurate in its quotes, statistics, and facts?
   Are names, addresses, product titles spelled correctly?
   Have all grammatical mistakes been corrected?
   Is the author consistent in handling headings, introduction of artwork, footnotes, beginning and ending of chapters, presentation of graphics, terms used for the same object?
   Do headings in the text correspond to those in the table of contents?
   How does the text look on the page?
3. On the revised final version:
   Have all the corrections you asked for been made——one way or another?

        Have any new errors crept in during the revision? Should there be any new changes in the way the material looks on the page?

4. On the approved final version for a printer:

        Has the writer specified how to set headings, running heads, page makeup, notes, prefatory and appended material?

        Has the writer labeled each of these elements in the text, so the printer will recognize them?

        Has the writer noted type size and font for regular text, italics, boldface, headings, titles?

        If you are giving the typesetter the disks or tapes from your word processor, have you taken out your codes and put in those that make sense to the typesetter's machine?

        Have you prepared a list of those commands, and what they mean, for the typesetter?

        If you have to correct little mistakes in this version, are you sure you're using conventional proofreaders' marks, so the typesetter will know what you mean?

When making notes for the writer, avoid some of the sins of teachers. Don't scribble "awkward" in the margin and leave it at that. Ditto for "expand," or "develop this." What do you mean? Take the time to imagine how the passage should or could look.

Don't say it's "nice," and nothing more. Why read it if that's all you're going to say? Don't completely rewrite whole paragraphs. Restrain yourself. How else is a weak writer going to learn? Certainly not by reading your perfect prose, and cursing.

Write what you think down. Don't leave it to the writer to figure it out from cryptic notes in the margin. Start with praise. (Most people think editing means criticizing. But no one will listen to an uninterrupted flow of attack. Find something worth approving.)

Then concentrate on large issues—problems that pop up throughout the manuscript, organizational issues. For example, you could say:

> # 1: You keep talking about our employees as "workers" (Pages 1, 13, 15, 17, marked), "laborers" (Pages 3, 13, 16, 21), and "union stiffs" (Page 20). But some of our employees are secretaries, supervisors, assemblers, inspectors. So let's just use the blander term, *employees.*

When you state your advice as a general principle at the beginning, you don't have to repeat it at every instance in the text. You can just refer back, like this:

TEXT:	*YOUR COMMENTS:*
. . . so I believe we should offer incentives to our union stiffs on a regular basis	employees (note #1)

Only when you've finished talking about the big problems should you bother discussing little details. I'd go through the manuscript page by page, writing comments about any correction you think the writer might not understand. For instance:

Page 13:

Payroll issues: Don't you think we should say something like "issues of salary and benefits" here?

Paragraph beginning "And so . . ." I don't get the transition here. Why does this follow?

> Paragraph beginning "Statistics show . . ." Shouldn't this go up on page 10? It seems to lead into the top of the page there. What do you think?

Your tone here can influence whether the writer will accept or reject your suggestions. You're not a theater critic lambasting last night's opening.

To make sure the writer understands that you're just *raising* issues, not offering final solutions, talk over the document with your critique at hand. Ask what the writer feels is best. Take back your outlandish suggestions (if you made any). Reach agreement on what you both think needs to be done.

Of course, after you've done all this, you and your staff may be sending out honest memos, straightforward letters, reports that anyone can understand. And that could cause you problems.

Some companies aren't used to plain talk. Some nervous managers—particularly at the middle level—respect only big fat paragraphs with passive constructions and no action recommended at the end. People like that may attack your staff for writing plain English.

Defend your people, then, to show them you mean what you say. Top management will usually back you up. Almost no one tells them anything, so they appreciate hearing the truth.

And after a while, when other people in the company send back praise for a report your staff turned out, make a point of circulating that, adding your own congratulations. But be prepared. Clear writing will bring your group more work. So dig in.

□ *Index* □